BEAZLEY AND OXFORD

BEAZLEY AND OXFORD

Lectures delivered in Wolfson College, Oxford, 28 June 1985

by

DIETRICH VON BOTHMER

MARTIN ROBERTSON

DALE TRENDALL

JOHN BOARDMAN

with

'Sir John Beazley (1885–1970)'

by

BERNARD ASHMOLE

Edited by

DONNA KURTZ

at the Beazley Archive

Monograph Number 10

Oxford University Committee for Archaeology

1985

Oxford University Committee for Archaeology

Monograph No. 10

Published by the Oxford University Committee for Archaeology
Institute of Archaeology
Beaumont Street
Oxford

Distributed by Oxbow Books
10 St. Cross Road, Oxford OX1 3TU

ISBN 0 947816 10 0

Typeset on a Monotype Lasercomp at the Oxford University Computing Service
Printed in Great Britain at the Alden Press, Oxford

CONTENTS

FOREWORD

JOHN DAVIDSON BEAZLEY was born on 13 September 1885. The centenary of his birth was celebrated in London and Oxford with colloquia on Greek Vases. Although Beazley's scholarship encompassed very many aspects of classical art and literature, it was best known and most influential in the study of Greek Vases. The colloquium in London,('Greek Vase-Painters') was sponsored by the Greek and Roman Department of the British Museum. The Oxford colloquium ('Beazley and Oxford') was sponsored by the Beazley Archive; it took place in Wolfson College and also celebrated the centenary of the Lincoln Professorship.

This volume publishes the Oxford colloquium and reprints, with the permission of the British Academy, the fullest account of Beazley's life, the obituary prepared for the Academy by his friend, colleague and successor to the Lincoln Professorship, Bernard Ashmole. There is also a brief account of the establishment and development of the Beazley Archive.

The four Oxford papers were delivered by Dietrich von Bothmer, Martin Robertson, Dale Trendall and John Boardman, all of whom knew Beazley and worked with him. Dietrich von Bothmer is the only one of the four who was a student at Oxford and a pupil of Beazley. After completing undergraduate studies in Berlin he came to Oxford as a Rhodes Scholar for one year to take a Diploma in Classical Archaeology. From Oxford he went to the United States, where he received a doctorate from the University of California at Berkeley, then to the Metropolitan Museum in New York. Throughout the long years of his association with that museum, he has been able to travel widely and to engage regularly in the close personal examination of objects which is vital to classical archaeologists. In later years Beazley could not make study-trips and Dietrich could assist his teacher by providing information about collections which he could no longer visit. Beazley's gratitude for this knowledge shared is generously acknowledged in the prefaces to his monumental lists of Attic black- and red-figure vase-painters.

Martin Robertson, like Dale Trendall and John Boardman, studied at Cambridge University, not Oxford. His parents knew Beazley well. Martin met him as a child, and when he first went to Greece as a young graduate Beazley recommended him to his favourite pupil, Humfry Payne, then director of the British School at Athens. Martin's love for Greece flourished and his association with Beazley became close. Many of us would say that he most nearly approaches

1

Beazley in sensitivity, selflessness and style. With characteristic modesty he concealed his great personal contribution to *Paralipomena* with the words, 'for the final state I am responsible'. With his predecessor in the Lincoln Professorship, Bernard Ashmole, and his successor, John Boardman, the Beazley Archive has had the best possible guidance.

Dale Trendall came to Cambridge University from New Zealand. His life has been spent circling the world in the study of South Italian vases, while holding a succession of distinguished academic posts in Australia. The choice of South Italian vases was his own but the model which he followed was the one Beazley developed for Athenian vases and taught his pupil Noël Oakeshott (née Moon). She lived in Oxford and shared a life-long interest in South Italian vases with him and Dale who came to Oxford as often as his work permitted. Her husband, Walter Oakeshott, was Vice-Chancellor when the University of Oxford purchased Beazley's archive.

John Boardman, Lincoln Professor of Classical Archaeology and Art, was an undergraduate at Cambridge. Although he was not a pupil of Beazley, he has devoted a portion of his career as field-archaeologist, museum curator and teacher to what might be called Beazley Studies. The first night he spent in Oxford was as Beazley's guest at 100 Holywell Street. He has been actively involved in major scholarly enterprises outside Oxford and outside England, but his closest association is with the University of Oxford now celebrating 100 years of classical archaeology.

In addition to the colloquia in London and Oxford the Beazley Centenary was marked by exhibitions in Sotheby's Main Galleries ('Beazley Drawings') and in the Ashmolean Museum ('Beazley and Oxford').

The Beazley Archive wishes to acknowledge the co-operation and support over many years of the Ashmolean Museum and Library, the Faculty of Literae Humaniores, Lincoln College (Shuffry Fund), the Meyerstein and Craven Funds, the University Computing Service, the British Academy, the Fitch Foundation, and, from the summer of 1984, the J. Paul Getty Trust. We would also like to express thanks to those who assisted with the centenary celebrations, especially Brian Cook and Dyfri Williams (British Museum), Felicity Nicholson and Oliver Forge (Sotheby's), Ian Blake and Peter Attenborough (Charterhouse School), Bernard Ashmole, Herbert Cahn, Jasper Griffin and Hugh Lloyd-Jones, Walter Oakeshott and Nigel Wilson, Balliol, Christ Church and Lincoln colleges, the President, Fellows and staff of Wolfson College, also Elie Borowski, Nicolaos Embiricos, Karl Schefold, and the Morat Institut (Basel). Ruth Glynn kindly supervised the production of the text of this book.

A subject index to Beazley's published work, and a bibliography, compiled by Martin Robertson, will be published by the Beazley Archive.

The notes, drawings and photographs with which Beazley worked were purchased by the University of Oxford in 1964. Excellence is not uncommon in Oxford but monetary recognition from within the University is rare. The purchase of the material was a gesture of unusual generosity to a scholar who had won the respect of the University, and a means of securing the greater comfort of Beazley's last years. Until his death in 1970 the prodigious mass remained in his home, 100 Holywell Street. Then it became necessary to move the material to the only space available in the Ashmolean Museum. Bernard Ashmole gave a research student (now the Beazley Archivist) the task of ordering it. With the help of Martin Robertson and John Boardman, they transferred the material, attempting to discern order in the papers and photographs which had fallen into disorder during the last years of Beazley's life when he was too frail to look after them properly.

The Archive which the University purchased was created by one man for his personal use. The immediate task, after the preliminary sorting of the more than 100,000 photographs by material (sculpture, bronzes, terracottas, vases, etc.), was to devise a system which would enable the bulk of the vase material (the 'unique' and most valuable part of the collection) to be consulted by a large number of people so as to become a research centre for the study of Greek vase-painting. In addition to photographs, a significant portion of which Beazley had mounted and labelled with attributions, the vase-material included hundreds of thousands of notes, neatly transcribed on sheets of paper in a virtually indecipherable shorthand, and about two thousand drawings traced off the surface of vases. The drawings are more informative to those who wish to pursue the connoisseurship of the vases than the highly personal notes. Beazley was not keen to explain his method and his most influential publications are monumental lists of vases ordered by artists and groups.

Since 1970 the Archive has been available to students, senior scholars, museum curators, dealers and private collectors, and has been consulted on a wide range of subjects which is by no means restricted to problems of attribution. During these years the number of photographs in the collection has increased by about fifty percent. Some were purchased on a small university annual grant but many were given by scholars in gratitude for the Archive's services and in the hope that it would flourish. Much of the Archive's work is done through correspondence but large numbers of people have been drawn to Oxford, to study for a day or years in the ideal intellectual environment of the Ashmolean Library.

The international cohesion of the subject which Beazley's unrivalled scholarship had assured was in serious danger during the first decade of the Archive's existence. Making the material available was a laudable aim but something more was required to ensure that his work was carried on; the published lists needed to be revised and augmented as Beazley himself had done. Scholars were invited to contribute information to the Archive which could disseminate it effectively. During these years the application of computers to art history became more generally acknowledged, and in 1979 the Archive decided to embark on a computerized inventory of all known Athenian black- and red-figure vases. Beazley's lists were comprised of regularized segments of information (e.g. museum, inventory, shape, technique, artists, provenance, subject, publication) which could be adapted to computer 'fields' without altering his principles of classification and attribution in any way. In 1982 the Archive published *Beazley*

Addenda (compiled by Lucilla Burn and Ruth Glynn) which brought up to date references to illustrations of vases attributed by Beazley. Documentation on vases which Beazley either did not assign or did not know has also been compiled in readiness for future publications. In 1984 the Archive published the *Summary Guide to CVA* (compiled by Tom Carpenter) as a by-product of its research project.

In the year of Beazley's Centenary the Archive is an international research centre to which information can be entrusted for accurate and impartial recording and from which it can be widely and generously disseminated. It is a centre which welcomes established scholars *and* young students, and one which instructs the latter in Beazley's methods and standards of scholarship. The Archive can look forward with confidence to a future of greatly increased capabilities and services. Its database, demonstrated by telephone link with the Oxford University Computing Service (to which we owe boundless thanks for patient co-operation and excellent advice, especially to Lou Burnard and Susan Hockey) to the Second International Conference on Automatic Processing of Art History Data and Documents held in Pisa in September 1984, is already generally acknowledged to be one of the most highly developed in the art world. We have before us the potential of modern high technology and behind us a well established tradition, and a photographic archive of unparalleled richness. We think Sir John Beazley would be pleased.

Summer 1985   *Donna Carol Kurtz*

BEAZLEY THE TEACHER

Dietrich von Bothmer

METROPOLITAN MUSEUM OF ART, NEW YORK

LET me explain at the outset, that the printed title of this talk, 'Beazley the Teacher', was not chosen by me. I should have preferred 'Learning from Beazley', as possibly more descriptive of what I can safely talk about, the more so since Beazley toward the end of his life confessed to me that he had never enjoyed class room instruction. Nor am I truly qualified to comment on 'Beazley and Oxford', the general title of today's colloquy. For one thing, my own attendance at Oxford was all too short—the three terms of the academic year 1938/39—and I merely 'satisfied the Examiners in the Examination for the Diploma in Classical Archaeology in Trinity Term, 1939', to quote the University Registry. If I talk today at all about Beazley it is in order to express publicly my thanks for the thirty years in which I have been fortunate enough to learn from Beazley while he was still with us, and in order to explain to this learned audience how much all of us can still learn from Beazley now that he is no more.

The first lesson I received from Beazley took place on my first day at Oxford, Thursday 6 October 1938. American students are somewhat pampered by 'college advisors' and 'counsellors' at American Universities and are apt to have difficulties adjusting to Oxford with its mixture of apparent informality and cultivated indifference. My difficulties were of a different nature. I was an undergraduate at Wadham, and Bowra told me that Jacobsthal would be my tutor and that I should see him forthwith. Map in hand I dutifully went to Christ Church, where Jacobsthal in turn told me that Beazley was expecting me at the Ashmolean. There F. Tandy, the lanternist, informed me that I should wait outside the door of the Library for Beazley to come out and to see me. Not even knowing what Beazley looked like, I expected the first gentleman who looked like a professor to be Beazley. Presently the door opened, and I introduced myself, but the gentleman I accosted was not Beazley but K.T. Parker, and after a short exposure to Old Master drawings, I was told by the Keeper with a chuckle: 'Oh, you must want to see Beazley', and it was Parker who personally conducted me to the table in the Library where Professor Beazley was busily excerpting the latest volume of *Monumenti Antichi*. He looked up, turned around and asked me what I intended to do at Oxford. I replied that I should like to work on the Antiphon Group sorting out those vases that were not by the painter of the name-piece, alluding to Beazley's preamble in *Attische Vasenmaler des rotfigurigen Stils* (p. 230), in which he

5

had said, 'Ich möchte gern das ausscheiden, was sicher von dem Maler des schönen Untersatzes (Nr. 1) gemalt ist, doch will mir das noch nicht gelingen'.

Beazley looked at me quizzically and asked: 'How old are you?' When I informed him, 'Nineteen, going on twenty', he drily replied: 'You will find instruction at Oxford very elementary, and, besides, I have already done what I couldn't do in 1925 in my new book, now almost ready to go to the printer'. Needless to say I was mortified, but the lesson, so elegantly administered, sank in.

There was much to learn and absorb in those three terms at Oxford. Beazley lectured on Greek Sculpture and on Greek Vases, but in addition there were what Beazley called his private classes, conducted in the galleries of the Ashmolean in which the two or three of us reading for the Diploma in Classical Archaeology were exposed to bronzes, terracottas, and gems. Nothing, of course, was taken out of the cases, but even through the glass we were taught how to look and what to look for. The most rewarding, and at the same time most informal (or should I say 'least structured'?) sessions were those conducted by Beazley at home on Friday afternoons. We met at 4 o'clock for tea at 100 Holywell, with Professor and Mrs Beazley and any other guests who happened to be there in what was then still a dining room, before it housed the overflow of notes and photographs. During tea Beazley remained totally silent, obviously deep in thought, but at 5 o'clock sharp he rose and conducted us to the adjacent study where for two hours we were shown photographs and fragments of vases, which we were allowed to handle. Looking back at this experience after nearly half a century, the physical exposure to the objects, introduced so casually, was easily the most rewarding aspect. It was on these Friday afternoons that Beazley asked us questions, and I shall never forget his uncanny prescience of our ignorance and the gentle way in which he filled the gaps in our knowledge. To the three levels of learning from Beazley, his courses of lectures, his gallery talks in the Ashmolean, and his seminars conducted at home, I must add a fourth source, his conversations. Every working day, almost from the very beginning of Michaelmas Term 1938, Beazley would get up from his seat in the Library shortly before one o'clock and ask me: 'Are you going back to Wadham?' and I would accompany him not just to the corner of the Kings Arms but, of course, all the way to 100 Holywell. On these walks Beazley would talk freely and invited questions, and there were very few topics that he did not broach. My mistakes in English were caught and corrected, but so encouragingly that I did not despair of ever learning this foreign tongue. His voice was so clear and his enunciation so free of the so-called Oxford accent that it was a pleasure to learn from his way of expressing himself, and there was always humour in his remarks—difficult to catch at first, but so consistent as to become infectious. Beazley was one of the very few scholars I have known who wrote as he spoke and who spoke as he thought, with the simple precision based on an extraordinary knowledge coupled with a severe discipline; for those of us who remember him it has also been especially rewarding to read him with the cadence of his speech in mind.

When I left Oxford in June of 1939 to visit museums in America Beazley kindly gave me a letter of introduction to L.D. Caskey at the Museum of Fine Arts in Boston, and the warm reception I got in Boston showed that being accepted and recommended by Beazley immediately gained admission to the large circle of his many friends and disciples. That summer of 1939 began my long correspondence with Beazley and set the pattern of countless letters supplying Beazley with information on new vases, changes of numbers, or detailed descriptions and sketches of obscurer points, a correspondence to which Beazley always replied cogently and courteously. When the suspension of the Rhodes Scholarships for the duration of the war prevented my return to Oxford, it was therefore doubly fortunate that I was given the chance to continue studying at the University of California in Berkeley under H.R.W. Smith, himself a pupil of Beazley's, who though separated from Oxford by thousands of miles had not only kept in touch with his former teacher but applied to his students the same training he had received many years before. Roy Smith had written a doctoral dissertation at Princeton University on the Menon Painter, and the unstinted praise that Beazley bestowed on the published version in one of his rare fully positive reviews of that period (*JHS* 51 (1931) 119−20) is worth quoting in part:

> It is a very good study: it shows not only great patience and precise knowledge, but also a rare feeling for distinctions and delicacies of style: moreover in spite of all its curious detail, it reads easily, and amusingly, and excitingly; for Mr Smith is one of the not very many English-speaking archaeologists who can write, and are not content to exude or secrete.

This judgement reveals in many ways what Beazley valued in archaeologists and, in a sense, sums up the standards he applied to himself. Though reluctant to explain his method in his own writing, by indirection, in the praise of others, he clarified his own views, as when he says of Smith in the same review:

> He has pored over every line in them [i.e. the vases by the Menon Painter], not once but many times: and that is the only way; far-view must be supplemented by close-view; the two ultimately blend, and become familiarity with the vase, knowledge of the vase, understanding of the vase.

To be accepted by Beazley, not to disappoint him, and to maintain the standards sometimes only divined, became the guiding principle of Smith's life and work. Cut off from Europe during the war, the next best thing to learning from Beazley in person on daily walks from the Ashmolean to Wadham, was surely to see his training carried on, transplanted Κιμμερίων ἀπὸ γῆς χῶρον ἐς Ἑσπερίδων, to quote from Beazley's Greek dedication of *Development of Attic Black-figure* to his friend H.R.W. Smith.

Isolated though life in California can sometimes be, and doubly so in wartime, this enforced ἀναχώρησις had its distinct advantages in encouraging the reading and rereading of everything Beazley had published. And by everything I mean literally everything, even such relatively obscure papers as the one delivered at the University of London Conference on the Future of Archaeology in August 1943 which, though published, does not appear in the two published Bibliographies of Beazley. His paper under the heading 'University Training' spells out precisely on little more than two pages his views, which not surprisingly concentrate on learning rather than teaching. The ten particulars he enumerates should be taken as the ten commandments and cover just about every aspect to which a young student should address himself. The first item in this decalogue reads: 'He should spend as much of his time as possible with *originals* rather than with pictures of them in books.'

His conclusion, even more valid today than in 1943, is worth quoting in full:

> It is sometimes thought that the museums have been *worked through*, and that for fresh light on ancient art and archaeological problems the world is dependent on new excavations. Our student will not be of this opinion, but will realise that from the enormous stores of objects already above ground, secrets incalculable in number and importance can be won by keen and patient scrutiny. He will also not think that a subject has been 'killed' because some other investigator has just made great progress, but rather that he has been provided with an incomparable springboard for fresh discoveries.

Whatever Beazley preached he applied to himself with enviable determination. Far from going into hibernation during the long, dark years of the war he patiently went through all the volumes of the *Annali* and the *Bolletino dell'Instituto* and extracted countless proveniences of vases, a labour that led to his spectacular reconstruction of the Brygos Tomb at Capua (*AJA* 49 (1945) 153 – 158): it would have pleased him immensely to see the transformation of his written account into the instructive exhibition that the British Museum has had the imagination to undertake this year. The same enforced perusal of old excavation accounts heightened his interest in Etruscan vase-painting. A chapter in *La Raccolta Benedetto Guglielmi nel Museo Gregoriano Etrusco*, published by the Vatican in 1939, had already demonstrated the astonishingly wide horizons of Beazley's perception and interest and had laid the groundwork to his monograph *Etruscan Vase-painting*, the second in the new Beazley and Jacobsthal series published at Oxford as *Oxford Monographs on Classical Archaeology* in 1947, for which addenda appeared in 1950 in the *Annuario della Scuola Archeologica di Atene* and a postscript 'Gleanings in Etruscan Red-figure' in *Festschrift Andreas Rumpf* in 1952.

Early in 1946, after the end of the war, Miss Richter persuaded the Director of the Metropolitan Museum in New York to invite Beazley to deliver the Arthur Gillender lectures in the Museum. He arrived on the *Aquitania* in Halifax on August 16th, civilian shipping still being difficult and based on priorities. Beazley came without his wife for whom transatlantic transportation could not be arranged. He stayed three months in North America, visiting Princeton, Philadelphia and Baltimore, New Haven, Boston and Worcester, as well as Toronto. I was able to work with him in Boston and Worcester and, of course, saw him daily while he was in New York: these months with Beazley were the first of my post-doctoral annual summer-sessions with him which lasted until the last years of his life.

Seeing Beazley outside Oxford added another dimension to my understanding of him, for he was no longer the Oxford instructor and examiner, but the older colleague and friend whom I could ask many a question and with whom I could share many an answer. In the early post-war years his deafness did not present an insuperable obstacle, and even later, as his hearing deteriorated, communication was not impossible. Scratch-pad and pencil were all one needed to avoid serious misunderstandings, and one learned, moreover, to be concise. His mind was such that a few key words would tell him at once the scope and area of the topic on which one wished to be enlightened. His deafness also made me a better listener, for as Bernard Ashmole so aptly put it in the obituary for *The Proceedings of the British Academy* (reprinted below), there were, indeed, very few subjects in which one could not learn from Beazley. These annual visits after 1946 were by no means limited to Oxford. In 1949 Beazley returned to America, this time accompanied by Lady Beazley, and once again I was with him in New York and Boston. 'Beazley and Museums' would have been another suitable contribution to the Centenary Colloquia, for seeing him at work in the Metropolitan Museum, the Brooklyn Museum, the Museum of Fine Arts in Boston, at the Fogg Museum in Cambridge, and in Worcester Massachusetts, as well as in London, both in the British Museum and the Victoria and Albert, at Reading, in the Louvre, in Athens, and in Ferrara has taught me more than any museum training course could ever accomplish. Add to this, shared visits to collectors like Captain E.G. Spencer-Churchill in Northwick Park, Walter Baker and Christos Bastis in New York, or the dealers in London, Paris, and New York that are no longer with us—Rudolf Forrer, Joseph Brummer, Jacob Hirsch, Hagop Kevorkian, and Jean Mikas, and you can begin to appreciate the advantages such an apprenticeship brought with it. Not content with objects already known or published, Beazley was always attracted by all he had never seen before. What he had not chanced on in his many travels, was often sent to him in the form of notes and photographs, and Beazley never failed to acknowledge these. Grateful for the opportunities he had received in his youth, especially at the hands of E.P. Warren and John Marshall at Lewes House, of studying material not yet published or visible to ordinary museum visitors, Beazley always shared his knowledge of objects, dates, location, interpretation, and attribution with all scholars, even the very young, who, he felt, would profit from such information. Wilhelm Kraiker's article on Epiktetos (*Jahrbuch* 44 (1929) 141−97) is perhaps the earliest proof of Beazley's generosity, and Miss Haspels' indispensable *Attic Black-figure Lekythoi*, published in 1936, is surely the most revealing monument of Beazley's help to a deserving disciple, who had studied under him at Oxford in 1928 and 1930.

How did Beazley acquire his phenomenal knowledge and how did he organise it for instant retrieval? In his early years he filled copy books on his visits to museums, but he soon devised a loose-leaf system, in which each object that he saw and studied had its own sheet or sheets of the standard foolscap size, sheets that were then sorted and piled on shelves. The sorting was, in the case of vases, done by painters, and within the painters by shapes, corresponding more or less to the sequences established in his published lists of painters. Notes on unattributed vases were often next to attributed ones, if Beazley felt there was a kinship, even if not strong enough to warrant an entry in one of his published lists. Other unattributed vases were simply arranged by shape. While at work in museums, Beazley, to save paper, would enter several objects on the same page, but on his return home these

notes were then transcribed. Tracings of vases and sketches often accompanied
these notes, and the tracings were merely slipped in next to the descriptive pages to
which they pertained. The notes were done in pencil, sometimes rather blunt,
written with a light hand, and employing abbreviations that are not always easy to
decipher. As soon as the first fascicules of the *Corpus Vasorum Antiquorum* were
published, Beazley decided to mount his photographs on thin cardboard sheets cut
by the Oxford University Press to the exact size of the *CVA* plates. Until the war
these cardboard mounts were tan in colour and of reasonably good quality; after
the war Beazley was much distressed that the new cardboard was rather limp,
dark grey, and of a rough surface, which did not take ink nearly so well as the
earlier mounts.

It is perhaps useful to explain that in the old days it had not yet become the
custom merely to write or telephone a museum, without a letter of introduction, to
announce one's visit, and to request that certain objects be taken off exhibition
and carried to a study room or office for closer study. Most of the time one was
happy to see what was on view in the galleries and to take notes through the glass
of a case or vitrine, though in some museums even this harmless occupation was
not allowed. On Beazley's first visits to the Villa Giulia, note-taking was strictly
prohibited, and Beazley had to leave the galleries and go outside the museum
every time he wanted to jot down what he had just seen and remembered. He
became so good at this practice of committing to memory what he could not write
down in front of the object, that toward the end of his first study trip to Rome, he
did not have to leave the museum after every vase that he had absorbed, but could
recall correctly between eight and ten vases before dashing out to write up his
notes. As to visiting storerooms, this, of course, was out of the question. In
Beazley's publication on the Villa Giulia Painter (*RM* 27 (1912) 286–97) some
echoes of his difficulties can be sensed: not only is the name-piece not illustrated,
there is no acknowledgement to the authorities of the Villa Giulia. It was not until
1929 that Beazley saw the Castellani fragments in the Villa Giulia. He at once
recognised joins with the Campana fragments in Florence that he had already
studied in 1912, thanks to Antonio Minto, and his enthusiasm for the task in hand
must have rubbed off on the museum authorities, resulting in the monograph
Campana Fragments in Florence (1933), the preface of which spells out the facts in
precise detail.

Beazley had the happiest memories of these painstaking labours in Florence and
in the Villa Giulia. With his great knowledge and power of concentration, coupled
with an inborn attention to the smallest detail, work on fragments of vases was the
most exacting but also the most rewarding of the many tasks he had set himself.
The frontispiece of the *Campana Fragments*, restoring photographically an Oltos cup
now scattered among six different locations, has served as a visual reminder of how
to contribute to the study of vase-painting to many of his pupils and followers.
Beazley summed up his own approach in the review (*JHS* 53 (1933) 309) of
Kraiker's catalogue of red-figure vases in Heidelberg:

> Dr Kraiker is not of those who count time spent on fragments time frittered away: his catalogue shows not only the right care, but a nice feeling for distinction of style. Work on fragments exercises this sense and develops it.

Though in the Louvre working conditions for scholars in those distant days were somewhat better than in the Villa Giulia, they were far from ideal. Beazley had worked steadily since his undergraduate days at Oxford on the vases in the Louvre, but his approach and method of attributing vases were unfortunately not shared by Edmond Pottier, thirty years his senior. The world owes the creation of the *Corpus Vasorum Antiquorum* to Pottier who, at an age when most scholars think of their retirement, first proposed it in a long and detailed memorandum submitted to the Académie des Inscriptions et Belles-Lettres on 28 December 1919 (which was unanimously adopted by the Union Académique Internationale in 1920). Pottier really loved vases, and the continual corrections that Beazley printed in his reviews of his Louvre fascicules between 1923 and 1933 may well have been felt by the originator of the new series as a criticism of the *Corpus* as such, an undertaking of his in which Pottier understandably took considerable pride.

Just as Beazley's reception in the Villa Giulia changed for the better with his discovery of joins between the Campana fragments in Florence and the Castellani fragments in Rome, the same change in his fortunes came about in the Louvre, after Pottier's death in 1934, through a fragment in Florence that supplied the back of Dionysos's head on the Berlin Painter's amphora acquired by the Louvre in December 1934. Beazley noted the join, and Michon and Merlin of the Louvre not only saw to it that through an exchange with Florence the fragment was incorporated in the Louvre vase, but invited Beazley to write up the vase jointly with Merlin for the *Monuments Piot* (35 (1935 – 1936) 49 – 72). Beazley, in later years, would not fail to remark while passing the big vitrine in which the amphora is exhibited in the Louvre, that thanks to the small fragment in Florence from that moment on he was no longer considered a *farceur* by the Louvre.

Beazley always insisted that the best way to be received in a museum was to do something for the institution visited, not to guard one's discoveries *in pectore* but to share them freely. He was also always punctilious in acknowledging favours that he received in his labours: who can forget the warm words addressed to Pierre Devambez and Nereo Alfieri in his preface to the second edition of *ARV*, or the thanks rendered in the preface to the second Oxford fascicule of the *Corpus* to D.B. Harden 'who opened and closed the cases for me day after day'.

At this point you may well ask whether I have not strayed from the subject and merely given you reminiscences and anecdotes, but some of you may have gathered that the extraordinary range of Beazley's knowledge and the keen interest he took in so many aspects of life and learning were such an essential part of his existence that they cannot be ignored. And learning is so different from studying for an examination, or taking a degree, that any attempt to learn from Beazley must be based not only on his published writings, but on the example of his life, his outlook, or, if you wish, his philosophy. The staggering body of his attributions somehow overshadows his real accomplishment, which is the elevation of vase-painting to an artistic recognition, not at all current when he began. The German 'Kleinkunst', though not in itself pejorative, becomes in English 'minor arts', and the prejudice attached to this categorisation is one from which students of my generation had to suffer until fairly recently. Beazley changed all this, not by lofty proclamations, but by his steady industry and his persuasive personality. His zeal was infectious, and even before the publication of his first book, *Vases in America*, the *Museum Journal* (5 (1914) 175) of the University Museum in Philadelphia reported Beazley's visit of 1914, in the following terms:

> J.D. Beazley, Esq. of Christ Church, Oxford, visited the museum early in September and spent several days in studying the collection of Attic red-figured vases. Mr. Beazley's studies in this field of art have convinced him of the possibility of assigning Attic vases to their respective artists.

That this was indeed his firm belief is proved by the simple lines of the preface to *Vases in America*:

> I deal primarily with the red-figured vases in United States Museums: I have tried to find out who painted each. I have not been able to assign every vase to its author, although I do not consider that an impossible task, but I have managed to put in place most of the more, many of the less, important pieces.

Terser yet, though not meant to be boastful, is his own comment on *Attische Vasenmaler des rotfigurigen Stils* in the bibliography of Beazley and Ashmole, *Greek Sculpture and Painting* (1932): all he says is 'the vases assigned to their painter'.

In the preface of his German book he also cautioned the reader, and I paraphrase: 'Since the appearance of *Vases in America*, or rather since writing it, I have changed my mind here and there, but', he added, 'nobody accustomed to working continuously in a field of study would reproach me for this, and, besides, such changes of opinion are neither numerous nor do they affect the essentials.'

Here we see expressed a caution that comes with maturity. In his first book, *Vases in America*, he had declared with great conviction: 'The Attic vase-painter possessed a highly individual style. However obscure he may be, the artist cannot escape detection if only sufficiently delicate tests be applied. It was hard, at first, I remember to distinguish the Syriskos Painter from the Painter of the Copenhagen amphora, or even the Villa Giulia Painter from the Painter of the Chicago stamnos. But now it is quite easy.'

I recalled the Syriskos—Copenhagen problem more than thirty years later when I informed Beazley of a fragment that I had acquired and tentatively attributed to the Copenhagen Painter. In my next letter, however, I wavered and thought it should instead be by the Syriskos Painter. Beazley, once he got the photograph, wrote as follows: 'It makes me think of the Copenhagen Painter. I have had difficulty again recently telling him from the Syriskos Painter in a fragment.' That Beazley on occasion changed his mind is not really so surprising as it might strike some of the younger students who have had to struggle with, for instance, his approach to the Andokides Painter and the Lysippides Painter. More dogmatic scholars would have kept their doubts to themselves, but such was the extreme intellectual honesty of Beazley that he did not mind recanting. 'Eating his words' he called it, and this took courage. What is perhaps not always clear to everybody is that an attribution changed by Beazley was never done on the spur of the moment, but the result of long scrutiny in which all the evidence was carefully weighed. Every day of his life, Beazley's knowledge increased, not only because of the wealth of new material that came to his attention constantly, but also because he forever widened his horizon; 'to be considered' was a phrase often used by Beazley in his correspondence, and he did not exaggerate when, in the preface to the second edition of *Attic Red-figure Vase-painters*, he stated simply and correctly: 'every piece has been considered many times'. Nor did he wish to be slavishly copied, and it was always possible to argue an attribution with him. What he did resent was being misquoted or misunderstood, and this infuriated him to the point of explaining his strict views first in *Attic Red-figure Vase-painters* of 1942, then in *Attic Black-figure Vase-painters*, a third time in the second edition of *ARV* in 1963, and he took the trouble of reprinting his instructions for use in *Paralipomena*.

If I dwell on this point at all, it is because all too often in the past seventeen years it has become increasingly fashionable to write monographs on vase-painters; but instead of making new attributions and integrating them in the painter's oeuvre as established by Beazley, the fun seems to be to take out some of the vases given by Beazley to the painter and to declare that they cannot be by him. Much energy is spent in this exercise. Sometimes, to be sure, a proper join between two fragments assigned by Beazley to two different hands compels us, as it would have forced Beazley, to declare one of the attributions made by him in error, and I can assure you that Beazley would have made such changes, once properly informed of the circumstances, with alacrity. As a preoccupation, however, a certain danger should not be dismissed. The total changes of valid reattributions do not amount to a tenth of one percent of all the vases assigned to their painters by Beazley; emphasising what is in the opinion of the many contemporary writers a mistake in Beazley would, I fear, reflect badly not on Beazley but rather on the dissenter. Beazley's preface of 1967 to the reprint of *Vases in America* enumerates in ten paragraphs what he called his errors. He concludes his new preface with a single sentence that, I dare say, has no equal in archaeological literature: 'I regret these errors bitterly; compared with the vast number of correct attributions they are few.'

Until his mid-forties Beazley was filled with the optimism of the young, both as regards his projects and their speedy completion. In a letter to Miss Richter written on 14 March 1912 he spoke of his book which later became *Vases in America* as going to be finished in the summer. In a letter to Caskey of November 1914 he announces:

> I have written my text once, and am rewriting it which takes twice as long. I hope it won't require a third writing and that it will be ready by January, when I am going to become a kind of soldier. I shan't be sent to camp till the late spring, at any rate.

On June 20 of 1915 he reported again to Caskey:

> My book was finished in March, but the Oxford Press after promising to take it, refused. It is true that it turned out to be twice as long as I had originally thought. Now I am going to get an estimate for it and publish it if I can at my own expense; or at any rate contributing what proportion I am asked for, if it is not too much. I shall have money to spend in March next, as I have been made a proctor. We play strange parts in our time!

Half a year later, on 8 December 1915 he informed Caskey that: 'The Press has accepted my book but will not promise to publish it, it may be for years. They are short-handed.'

In the same letter he reveals his plans for what ten years later became *Attische Vasenmaler*: 'I have been working on my longer book Op. II and had hoped to get a skeleton ready before I have to stop, but doubt now if I can.' It was in response to this letter that Caskey suggested the Harvard University Press and on 5 February 1916 Beazley informed Caskey as follows:

> I went to the Press the other day and realised that my book would not be published till after the war. So I wrote to Chase sending particulars of it, this with the full approval of the Press which does not consider me in any way bound to it.

Two months later Beazley writes to Caskey from Boulogne where he had been assigned to the Censor's office at the Gare Maritime (3 April 1916):

> I am delighted that the Harvard Press is willing to publish my book, and very grateful to you and the others who have taken an interest in it. I am hoping Hoppin will be able to come to Boulogne and talk over this and other projects.

At the end of June of that year, still in Boulogne, he writes to Caskey in a happier vein:

> I hope to send off my pictures tomorrow. The text Hoppin took with him ... I shall be very glad when I have got the pictures off and when I hear they have arrived safely. They are going in the Embassy bag from London.

The experience with the Oxford University Press may have discouraged Beazley to submit another vase book to Oxford, and may help to explain why the second book, called Opus II in Beazley's letter to Caskey of 8 December 1915, was printed in Germany and in German. But his book on the gems in Warren's collection in Lewes House was printed by the Clarendon Press in 1920, as was *Greek Vases in Poland* in 1928. When enough new material had been accumulated to bring the German book up to date, Beazley had no hesitation to approach the Clarendon Press in the late 'thirties and went to some length and considerable financial sacrifice to indemnify the Tübingen publisher for his breach of contract. His thanks to the Clarendon Press for producing his first edition of *Attic Red-figure Vase-painters*, 'patriai tempore iniquo' is gratefully expressed in his preface, and elaborated after the death of John Johnson, Printer to the University, in the preface to the second edition, and he reciprocated the confidence shown to him by the Clarendon Press by remaining loyal to it to the end.

If the wealth of his writings and the enormous knowledge contained therein is self evident, the precise style of his publications conceals much of the agony that went into every work of his. The standards, of course, were self-imposed. Having circumnavigated in his youth entire continents he realised in middle life that he would also have to explore the dark interiors and put everything on his map if it was to be of use for others.

He freely gave vent to his moods in letters to me, from which I will quote some key passages. 10 November 1948: 'I have finished my Sather lectures: never have I earned money so hard'; and, a year later, 17 November 1949:

> I have been working at Attic Bf Vase-painters and have had much trouble. It is like going down a mine. Or reminds me of watching a diving competition when I was a little boy at school. The biggest boy remained an unconscionably long time underwater, and every one was sure he would fetch up all the pennies: but when at last he emerged he had found none.
>
> I make hardly any additions. It seems that if I do not know the painter of a vase when I see it I never know it now. The work so depresses me that I cannot turn to much else.

Or, still in the same vein, on Christmas Day 1949: 'Once in black-figure, one's boots stick in the mire ...'; and, on 23 September 1950: 'I have been working on the dregs of black-figure again which is depressing ...'
On 17 January 1951 Beazley reports:

> I am struggling to get Black-figure finished. I don't think I can add much more; but I have to spend some time on the Paris black-figure, and on the London, which is at present inaccessible owing to decoration of the rooms.

In addition to frequent complaints about the Haimon Painter and other lekythoi, there is also a telling passage about late eye cups (7 November 1950):

> I have done what I can to the eye-cups for *ABV*—not much, but I can now pass to something else. I cannot remember any class of bf vases I dislike so much, but others will occur.

Finally, in March 1952 he writes:

> I have more or less revised *ABV*, but I am always reminded of the Forth Bridge: you see a squad of men on it painting and you are told that the painting takes three years, and by the time they reach the far end it is time for them to start again at the near one.

Still, Beazley's sense of duty was such that he did not waver once he had set his course, and the same sense of a real obligation compelled him to carry the story of Attic red-figure down into the fourth century for his second edition of *ARV*.

At this time in his life lectures which he had composed with relative ease in the past—one thinks of *Attic Black-figure: a Sketch* for the British Academy; *Attic White Lekythoi* delivered at Newcastle on 1 November 1937; the Etruscan lecture at St Alban's in April 1944; or the *World of the Etruscan Mirror*, an Oxford lecture of 1947—became a burden to him which he did not conceal.

A good example is his lecture on Makron which he gave at the Classical meeting in Cambridge in August 1955 and repeated in Basle on 9 November 1956.

As early as 23 March 1955 he explained:

> After much hesitation, and rejection of other subjects, I chose to lecture on *Makron*. But now I find that although I am fond of Makron, there seems to be little to say about him (to a general audience) that has not been said already. This is one of the things I ought to have thought of before.

And two weeks later (8 April 1955) he confesses, still talking of the Makron lecture: 'I have reached the stage when it is as repugnant to me as bitter medicine to a small boy—absinthia taetra.'

The taste of Lucretius's 'bitter wormwood' is still with him when he writes in May:

> I have finished a rough draft of Makron; it seems to me miserable, and I despair of working it into anything presentable. With the trouble of Makron I have not been able to make any plans for the summer.

Ten days later he continues: 'The lecture on Makron is still troubling me, but I have made a second draft.' Early in July he reports, with some relief: 'I have more or less finished the lecture on Makron'; and finally, late in July: 'Next week the Congress. I have rehearsed my lecture and must now cut it down.'

There were, of course, other aspects to Beazley's productivity, the contributions he made gladly and cheerfully. It was Beazley whose gentle persuasion convinced his older friend Caskey to publish the finest red-figured vases in the Boston Museum of Fine Arts in the folio format of Furtwängler and Reichhold and who arranged for the printing by the Oxford University Press, supervising not only the preparation of the plates but advising Caskey on many matters connected with this splendid undertaking that was first conceived in August 1926. Caskey was not an aggressive optimist by nature, but Beazley's support expressed in letter after letter, and his offer to help swept away Caskey's scruples.

Of the many missives that crossed the ocean, Beazley's statement of 29 December 1926 is perhaps the most revealing. He wrote to Caskey as follows:

> A fascicule would be more use to scholars than half a dozen muddy fascicules of Corpus. Johnson (of the O.U.P.) has estimated for £200. His passage about me being responsible for passing of proofs means that you would trust me to pass them, instead of having them sent to America with expense for postage and especially delay. He also thought it would be a good thing if I could put some time in at the press when the things were actually being reproduced and printed. This I should most gladly do, and anything else to help the scheme on. And contribute of course, if you think that desirable.

This was an offer Caskey could not resist, and Beazley's help was fully acknowledged in the legend 'with the co-operation of J.D. Beazley' on the title page, when Part I was published in 1931. In the spirit of friendly rivalry between the Boston Museum of Fine Arts and the Metropolitan Museum of Art in New York that goes back to the beginning of this century, Miss Richter, who knew of

Caskey's project, planned a similar publication for the Attic red-figure in New York, and for many years Beazley was in lively correspondence with both Caskey and Miss Richter about the two publications. That there was never any hard feeling between the two Americans who both consulted Beazley will be readily understood by anybody brought up in the traditions of the 'twenties and 'thirties, and Beazley was able to help both, though fully aware of the differences between his two friends. His letter to Caskey of 22 July 1930 expresses his own judgement with his habitual tact and precision:

> Miss Richter has been here [i.e. at Oxford] and has talked to me about her publication of the New York vases. It ought to be very good—especially as it has yours to go on. It will have a didactic tone, lacking in yours, but that is quite a point of honour in New York.

Lacey Caskey died on 20 May 1944 after a long illness, and the task of finishing the Boston project fell to Beazley, now solely responsible for the text of Parts II and III. In accepting the invitation by the Trustees of the Museum of Fine Arts in 1944 to continue the vase publication, Beazley in the preface of Part II (published in 1954) spoke of it as the 'work of a friend and scholar whose mind and character I admired and from whom I had received much help and kindness through many years.'

Beazley as teacher in the wider sense can only be understood in terms of his extraordinary human qualities, his gift for friendship and sympathetic understanding, and measured by the high standards that he set for himself not only in the application of his scholarship but also in his daily conduct. If in his reviews of the last thirty years of his life he suppressed some of the scornful invective that had made him so feared a critic in his earlier decades, the change in tenor was not so much a mellowing of advanced years but prompted by a resigned tolerance of human errors. Gross mistakes in the works of colleagues, such as his wrong middle name in the entry about him in the Italian encyclopaedia of ancient art, were still noted by him, but instead of putting his correction in print, he merely reported them with wry amusement in his letters and conversation.

He became increasingly affected by the loss of many of his earlier companions and of his older colleagues and tutors, but he retained the capacity to make new friends, until the death of his beloved wife in 1967 brought on a despair and physical paralysis from which he did not recover.

Many of you will cherish your own memories of that remarkable man, recollections that will not always be identical in every particular with what I have tried to convey, but few will dispute the characterisation pronounced by this University at the Encaenia on 20 June 1956 when he was introduced to the Chancellor for admission to the D.Litt.:

Eum, qui sui prodigus semper fuit, numquam sui venditator.

BEAZLEY AND ATTIC VASE PAINTING

Martin Robertson

LINCOLN PROFESSOR 1961 – 1978

WE ARE here to celebrate the centenary of Beazley's birth, because we believe that his achievement, his contribution to our field of scholarship, is exceptional in its scope and in its effect on the study of Greek art; and that this effect has been for the good of the subject: both in enabling us to appreciate better the course of Greek art, the way in which the artists of Greece evolved a new approach to the representation of the visible world and so laid the foundations for European art; and in revealing to us the inter-related personalities of many great draughtsmen not recognised before. Certainly I believe this. I have worked all my life in the tradition established by Beazley and am convinced of its validity; and I suppose that that, more or less, is the view of most of us here.

There is, however, a different opinion: that Beazley's work, and the wide acceptance of his method, have had an essentially *bad* influence on the way our subject is studied; and I hope it will not be felt out of place if I devote this paper mainly to considering this view (or rather these views, for the attacks take independent and disparate forms); and if I approach them not simply in a polemical spirit of rebuttal or dismissal, though I think them essentially mistaken and hope to make points against them, but also trying to see what truths they may contain and what we can learn from them; for I think that there are such truths and such lessons.

I note parenthetically at this point that Beazley's great volumes of lists—*ABV*, *ARV* and *Paralipomena*—are sometimes jokingly referred to as the Bible; and this joke makes me a little uncomfortable. A bible, the unalterable text of a supposedly revealed truth, is something which can have no possible place in scholarship, where *every* scholar's every opinion must be provisional and revisable. A joke is a joke, certainly; but it may betray a dangerous attitude, and we need to remember that we can have no sacred books.

First, though, what exactly do we believe Beazley's special achievement to have been? Very briefly I suppose this: that by distinguishing the development of Attic vase-painting (black-figure, red-figure and white-ground) in terms of individual artists—master and pupil, colleagues and rivals, who learned from and influenced one another—he saved us from a schematic structure like that by which we distinguish the phases of Minoan or Helladic pottery; and instead we are able to watch the way in which the art was shaped by real men over three hundred years,

19

much as we can watch the way the painters of Florence or Siena or Venice shaped the progress of their schools over later centuries. Moreover, although it is clear from the written record that the major visual arts in Greece were no less dominated by personalities than on the one hand Greek literature and on the other the arts of the Renaissance; yet, owing to the still all but total loss of Greek painting on wall and panel and of Greek bronze statuary (finds of both in recent years give us wonderful glimpses but no coherent sequence) and the vast lacunae in what survives even of marble sculpture, the degree to which we can trace these arts in terms of personal styles relatable to surviving works is severely limited; so that the fact that we can do something of the sort in Attic vase-painting gives that an importance beyond itself.

The comparison of Attic vase-painting to Renaissance schools of painting carries grave dangers; and I am aware too that in this summary I have begged serious questions by the use of undefined terms, in particular 'art'. These are problems to which I shall come back, but now let us turn to the opposition.

I will start with the most recent assault, which is also the most comprehensive, that cleverly and forcefully launched by Michael Vickers. He has adumbrated his theory in various places, but I am most grateful to him for allowing me to read proofs of his forthcoming article in *JHS*,[1] where it is set out most fully and clearly. In a crude summary, Vickers's position is that potters have always been humble craftsmen, mass-producing ware in a cheap material, themselves and their products poorly regarded. It was only the arts and crafts movement of the later nineteenth century, a movement founded partly in puritanism, partly in reaction against mechanised production methods, that gave pottery a status as an art. Beazley, brought up in that atmosphere, wished the concept back on the Greeks, who would not have understood it and would have laughed at the notion of their pottery being highly esteemed; and by doing this he distorted our view of Greek art. I think that there is an element of truth in this proposition; and if so, it is something of importance which we clearly need to keep in mind. I will come back later to why I nevertheless believe that as a criticism of Beazley's work and its importance it is fundamentally irrelevant. Before that we must look at Vickers's own account of the character of Attic pottery. He recognises that black-figure, red-figure and white-ground are a peculiar phenomenon; and explains this by supposing that they are not a development taking place within the potters' tradition, but the result of a take-over by another and more prestigious craft, that of the silver and goldsmith. For the shapes and decoration alike of their vases these Attic potters (pot-makers and pot-decorators) are absolutely dependent on designs produced for gold and silver vessels. When the smiths had finished making silver and gold-ware for the rich, the designs they had used were passed on to the potters' shops where cheap clay versions were turned out for the tables of the poor. The orange colour of the clay was designed to look as like as possible to gold; the black to look like silver (tarnished, which was how, he claims, they liked it), the purple-red like copper; and the white like ivory; and not only 'like': where these colours occur on a clay vase they reproduce precisely (or as precisely as the poor hack of a potter could manage) the indications in the design for the disposition of the precious materials. Black-figure thus represents silver figures applied first perhaps on bronze, then on gold vessels, red-figure gold appliqués on silver. Since the workmen in the pottery had no status as original artists they cannot have put their names on vases, and the *egrapsen* and *epoiesen* inscriptions give those of respectively the designers and executors of the precious vessels, copied along with any other writing from the design to which the pot-decorator was working. (To account in this way for the *epoiesen* inscription one must suppose that the design was intended from the first for a particular executant.) The executant, being entrusted with the handling of the precious materials, held a more responsible and so a better paid position than the designer, which accounts for Euphronios moving from *egrapsen* to *epoiesen*.

Beazley's 'painters', distinguished by Morellian details of handling, are thus mere mechanicals, reproducing as best they can the designs of different artists but themselves in no real sense artistic personalities; and their products can be of interest to us only for the shadowy hints they give us of the lost masterpieces in silver and gold. The change from 'silver-figure' to 'gold-figure', reflected in that from black-figure to red-figure, was an economy measure, allowing the workers in precious metals to achieve their brilliant effects with the use of less gold and more silver; and this accounts for the triumph of the more difficult technique of red-figure over the easier one of black-figure.

The whole theory is integrated with another, a drastic down-dating of archaic art. I cannot go into that here; and it is not necessary, since, though the two theories can be used to support one another, the truth or falsehood of one is in no way dependent on the truth or falsehood of the other. The main importance of the chronological theory for the other is that it puts all the relevant material after the Persian wars, when there is evidence for an abundance of precious metals in Athens.

Since we have so very little external, independent evidence about the organisation of crafts in ancient Athens, an inclusive, monolithic, almost self-justifying theory like this is hard to prove absolutely wrong. If I say that to me it seems, in spite of many good points well made, as a whole utterly improbable, that is a personal opinion of no objective value. However, there are pieces of evidence of various kinds which can be adduced against some parts of it. For instance, in the fourth century we do have incontrovertible independent evidence in the form of two inscriptions on stone, which show that the names of Bacchios and Kittos, which occur with *epoiesen* on Panathenaic amphorae, were those of men engaged not in metal-working but in pottery.[2] True, this evidence concerns Panathenaic amphorae, for which we have other evidence that the vases of painted clay were the actual vessels in which the prize oil was given. Very likely clay was found a more suitable material for the storage of oil than metal; so these prize-vases are a special case. But this does not really resolve the problem. The black-figure designs on the Panathenaics are technically and stylistically indistinguishable from those on other painted pottery, and so, according to the theory, should be copied from designs for metal-work. Perhaps empty vessels of precious metal were given with the full clay ones, and their designs were copied by the potters; but then Kittos and

Bacchios should still be metal-workers, not the potters we know they were. Perhaps, in the special case of Panathenaics, the designers who normally supplied metal-workers sent their designs straight to the potters, who in such circumstances might feel justified in signing *epoiesen*. Perhaps; but, though the theory is not proved wrong by this evidence, it can only, it seems to me, digest it with difficulty.

Then there is the degree of real resemblance which the Attic pots may be supposed to bear to their conjectured metal models. I have not, I am afraid, been deeply into the question of whether and in what cases the Greeks liked silver tarnished. Obviously they did not always think of it that way. They did not, I suppose, picture Apollo with a black bow, still less Thetis or Aphrodite with black feet. The barefoot girl who passed the salley gardens may have been muddied to the ankle, but it was little snow-white feet that the lover saw, and so no doubt the goddesses' feet were envisaged. And though no doubt many Greeks had black teeth, a strip of silver behind the parted lips of a bronze statue is not, as Vickers himself remarks, intended to suggest that. Still, none of this would rule out a taste at a given time and place for tarnished vessels; and indeed Vickers produces some evidence for this. His fifth-century text, however, a quotation without context from a philosopher 'Silver is black',[3] may well be a deliberate paradox and so bear the opposite meaning to that claimed for it; and the later examples might reflect a taste for antiques looking antique, as one finds Roman copies in green basalt, showing a liking for the green patina on classical bronzes which their designers had certainly intended to be kept burnished. In any case, though, the most darkened silver would never look much like the glossy, positive black which Attic potters were evidently at such pains to produce. That the metallic sheen on many later black pots is not, as is sometimes suggested, a sign of technical decline but a deliberate attempt to emulate the appearance of metal, is I am sure true, and an important observation; but it does not prove that earlier black glaze was trying to look like tarnished silver; and if it were, the attempt was surely not very successful. Nor is the orange clay very like gold; and the practice, found in red-figure from the time of Euphronios, of occasionally adding details in real gold would have destroyed any illusion that the clay represented gold and surely shows that no such illusion was intended. Incision on black-figure is a technique which the vase-painter shared with and may have imitated from the metal-worker; but the black relief-lines and the golden-brown lines in diluted glaze with which the detail is put in on red-figure vases can have little to do with the appearance of 'gold-figure'. As to the undoubted fact that red-figure is a more difficult technique than black-figure, the notion that an artist-craftsman will never master a hard new technique in pursuit of a desired effect seems to me quite out of touch with reality.

The decoration of black ware presents similar problems. Silver vessels often have engraved decoration; and on many black vases elements of the design are incised in the clay before the black is applied, producing a similar effect, in so far as the black resembles silver; but it is curious that we do not seem to have any pottery vessels on which a figure is incised in the clay, reproducing the engraved figures found on fine silver-ware—easily imitated designs which would surely have been passed to the potters.

Then there is the question of shapes. Few people have denied, and those who have were surely foolish to do so, that Greek pottery shapes resemble metal shapes and were in some cases no doubt influenced by them. It seems to me likely, though, that the resemblance is more often a case of like ideals than of direct copying. It has been observed that vessels represented in pictures on black- and red-figure vases often differ in shape from anything we have in pottery. It is concluded that metal vessels are shown; surely rightly; but it is the *difference* from known pottery shapes that makes this conclusion plausible, so this is an argument against the idea that pottery shapes are servilely copied from metal ones. The Greeks in all their arts liked clearly delineated and sharply offset forms, and they were not troubled by the sentimental modern concept of 'truth to material'. There are Attic shapes which I would suppose to be based directly on metal models—the rhyton, for example, where the metal shape is itself derived, as John Boardman reminds me, from humble horn; and the kantharos is never a regular shape in Attic fine pottery, so probably when an Attic potter wanted or was asked to produce one, he looked to metal models. Similarly, early clay volute-kraters are rare and not uniform, and one readily supposes that the makers of those too looked to metal. About the time that red-figure was invented it does become a regular shape in fine pottery. According to the new theory this must be because only then did it become a popular form with gold- and silver-smiths. I would rather suppose that it was only then that potters became interested in it and made it one of their regular lines. This obviously cannot be decided either way; but consider the cases of the calyx-krater and the bell-krater. The earliest calyx-krater, that from the Agora ascribed to Exekias,[4] is strikingly heavier and simpler in its forms than the shape soon became, the various elements less sharply set off from one another, less 'metallic' one might say. The bell-krater is even more striking. The earliest, or at least the earliest complete examples we have, the footless lug-kraters decorated by the Berlin Painter,[5] are among the least 'metallic', the simplest and heaviest designs in Greek pottery; while the shape as it developed later has all the sharp articulations and offsets which make us think of Attic pottery as metallic. In these two cases we can surely see Attic potters inventing shapes, or if not inventing, then adapting them, not from metal but from rough kitchen pottery or from wood, and then refining them in the direction of the sharply articulated ideal which they shared with metal-workers. Metal calyx- and bell-kraters no doubt were made, but only I suppose later, borrowed from the potters whom we can clearly see developing them.

Mutual influence between crafts was surely widespread and various. Vickers cleverly argues for white lekythoi being copied from a shape in ivory which was a section of a tusk. By conventional dating the earliest examples of the shape which have a white slip are much later than the shape's invention, but here we come to the impasse of disagreement on dating. Attic alabastra in clay are often white, not (I would suppose) because they imitate ivory, but because the shape was originally an eastern one made in alabaster. Among white lekythoi, the late Group of the Huge Lekythoi is undoubtedly a poor man's version of the painted marble tombstone in lekythos-form popular at the time.[6] These, like the marble lekythoi, loutrophoroi and choes carved in relief which stood on other tombs, derive their forms from actual vessels, whether, as I would suppose, the clay ones, or, in the other view, from the vessels in precious materials from which the clay ones themselves derive.

To assert as a law of nature that originality is always found in more expensive materials, imitation in cheaper, is quite arbitrary and in some cases manifestly mistaken. Indeed work in precious materials is generally, I believe, no less remote from the mainstream of art than is the humble craft of painted pottery. Fabergé was a talented manipulator of expensive substances, but his is not the most interesting or influential name in the art of his time, nor near it. He is a footnote in the history of art. Cellini was in demand as a goldsmith; but his great salt at Vienna, a technical tour de force, has nothing like the important place in the history of art that his big bronze Perseus holds. The rich like to keep some of their bullion in a pretty form, for pleasure or display, and sometimes they employ serious artists in this connection, but it is a sideline of art. But this word 'art'—what one really means by it, and how legitimate it is to use it in the context of archaic and classical Greece—is a serious and difficult question and one very relevant to this discussion, and we shall have to come back to it.

Most centrally important, though, for our enquiry is the question of the status of painted pottery in Athens, and how, or whether, one can really conceive of it being simply taken over by the industry in precious metals. No one, I think, has suggested that Geometric and Orientalising pottery was in this state of sub-servience: that the huge Geometric grave-amphorae stood on the tombs of poor folk, those of the rich being surmounted by vast vessels in gold or silver, or even in bronze, which were the models for the potters. Yet these enormous and elaborately decorated clay pots are very curious things, not easily paralleled in the pottery of other times and places; and if, as is surely the case, they were the work of potters working in their own tradition, not under any strong influence from another craft, they show Athenian pottery of their time as something exceptional. Their tradition is continued in the Orientalising period, through such pieces as the Polyphemus amphora from Eleusis,[7] to the earliest black-figure of the Chimaera-Nettos Painter[8] and that circle. These last, according to the new theory, are already under the new dispensation: slavish copies of the designs of the metal-workers who have taken control of the Kerameikos. It seems to me far more natural to regard these potters and vase-painters as carrying on the peculiar tradition of Athenian pottery and transmitting it to their successors—Kleitias and Ergotimos, Amasis, Exekias, Euphronios, Onesimos, and on down to the time of Bacchios and Kittos—pottery workers all, working to their own designs in their own technique, though undoubtedly influenced by, and for that matter influencing, the work of craftsmen in precious and base metals.

But what, in the last analysis, makes for me this schema convincing and the other not, is the character of the best red-figure and black-figure vase-painting itself; and here *the best* needs emphasising, because the proportion of, and relation of, the best to the rest is a very important question which I feel has been somewhat slurred by Beazley's method, as applied both by himself and by us his followers, and of which it is urgently necessary to take account. I shall come back to this shortly; for the moment let us consider the best. It seems to me that when I look at the best works of any of the best painters I clearly see an artistic personality which develops and changes but retains its individuality; and that this is quite incompatible with the notion that he is slavishly copying designs passed to him by others. In a few cases one can even see him changing the design himself as he goes along. For instance, on the beautiful white-ground cup in the British Museum with Aphrodite on a goose, the artist, whom we know as the Pistoxenos Painter,[9] sketched the goddess with a three-quartered face but modified it to a profile in the finished drawing. The most striking examples are in the work of the so-called Kleophrades Painter. On a neck-amphora in Harrow[10] he put a silen on either side, holding pieces of armour for their master Dionysos to wear in the battle against the giants. In general he followed his preliminary sketch closely; but on both sides he changed the positions of the arms and the objects held in the hands, rethinking his designs more than once. In a picture of a warrior's departure drawn, seemingly earlier in his career, on an amphora in Würzburg,[11] the same artist sketched on the left of the picture a civilian in a himation, no doubt the warrior's father, balancing the woman on the right; but in the final version he substituted an archer in oriental costume. Vickers notes this phenomenon parenthetically, and admits that it shows that 'a silver design does not necessarily lie behind every decorated pot'; but this really, I think, will not quite do. All these beautiful vases are works of great care and elaboration; and according to his clearly expressed view really fine vase-painting must be following the smiths' designs closely; when the potter relies on himself he can only produce coarse hackwork. That not many such radical changes have been noticed does not detract from the importance of those that have; but I would stress that I cite this evidence only as a small point confirming the belief which I derive primarily from observing the development of a considerable number of outstanding artistic personalities.

So, for me, in Attic vase-painting there are true artists, true works of art; but there are also a great many pieces to which I would not give that name; a great many distinguishable but undistinguished craftsmen whom I would not call artists. This distinction between fine art and everyday craft is a difficult one with a difficult history. For the moment I will merely assert that for me the vase which gives the Pan Painter his name is a work of art; those from which the Haimon Painter takes his are not. Of course all arts show enormous ranges of quality. There were hack painters in fourteenth- and fifteenth-century Florence, fifteenth- and sixteenth-century Venice; but they were professional painters. Here we come back to a point I touched on earlier: that the comparison between Attic vase-painting and Renaissance painting can be dangerously misleading; and the dangers need spelling out.

The verbal distinction between craft and fine art was not, I think, made before Dürer around 1500; but the way that Dante, two centuries earlier, writes about Cimabue and Giotto and the illuminators of Bologna and Paris, and compares their rivalries and jealousies with those in his own art or craft of poetry, makes it clear that he thought of them, and they of themselves, much more as we think of 'artists' than as we think of 'craftsmen'. In antiquity the distinction was never made verbally; but again it is evident from what we are told about Parrhasios and Zeuxis, Apelles and Protogenes, that they very consciously considered themselves special people, in just the way that artists have since the term was invented. It appears to me also that this attitude was beginning to crystallise already in late archaic and early classical Greece, as is indicated by the widespread habit of craftsmen signing their works, and in particular by such an inscription as Euthymides' trumphant expression of rivalry with Euphronios; and in this connection of course it is of no significance whatever whether these are the names of potters or of silversmiths.

From other angles, naturally, that is an important question. Vickers is surely right to stress that pottery is a humble craft, its material, and in consequence its products, vastly cheaper than bronze, itself vastly cheaper than silver and gold. Potters were there primarily to provide cheap household ware for a wide public, and the bulk of Attic black-figure and red-figure is just that and has little or nothing to do with fine art. This has led to a different line of attack on Beazley's methods, suggesting that they are applicable only to the better quality works. This is, I think, in simplified terms, the attitude of Wegner and his pupils in Münster. The first essay of this kind was Stähler's work on the Eucharides Painter, published in 1967.[12] Stähler accepted the existence of this artistic personality, to whom Beazley had by then ascribed over ninety red-figure vases, but allowed him only four certain and two doubtful pieces, accepting three more as related, from the same workshop. I do not find this solution satisfactory; but it reflects the existence of a real problem in treating Attic vase-painting as a whole as a fine art. Vickers's suggestion that it was only in the ambience of the arts-and-crafts movement that any pottery could possibly be so regarded is not quite right. Emil Braun, for instance, in 1849, publishing the first engravings of the François Vase,[13] though devoting most of his space to discussion of subject-matter, went out of his way to give very warm praise indeed to the drawing, not only preferring it to that on the big fourth-century red-figure vases of South Italy, at that time considered the acme of Greek vase-painting, but speaking in absolute terms of a masterpiece and comparing the scenes to the choruses of Aeschylus. Still, the heyday of Attic vase-painting studies does come at the beginning of this century, and Vickers's observations on the arts-and-crafts movement as a background for Beazley are well worth making.

From another angle, Beazley in his early articles is clearly working under the direct influence of Morelli and Berenson in their studies of Italian painting;[14] and he treats Attic red-figure too unquestioningly, I feel, as an entirely comparable field. His use of the word 'Master' for his anonymous painters is an example of this dependence; trivial perhaps but not entirely without significance. More serious is his isolation, in his Berlin Master article of 1911,[15] of a large group of vases described as school-pieces. He speaks of them as 'direct and conscious imitations' but does not explain how he envisages the 'school'. He must, I think, have had in mind a studio like that of Botticelli or Bellini, where apprentices and assistants produced works after the master's designs; or at least, if he had no such precise picture, he borrowed the term 'school-pieces' from that context. Little as we know about workshop-organisation in the Kerameikos, this cannot be quite a true picture. Not a totally false one either: I suppose each workshop did have one or two leading decorators and others who learned their craft and took their style from the leader or leaders, and in some cases a master-pupil relation seems to me incontrovertibly established: the Achilles Painter, for instance, learning from the old Berlin Painter and in his turn teaching the Phiale Painter; but the context of a continuous demand for more or less mass-produced pottery on which figure-decoration is an expendable adjunct makes a very different ambience from that of a quattrocento painter's studio. Pottery is required in the first instance for some utilitarian purpose, whether as tableware or for ritual at a grave, or something else; its decoration is a secondary matter. Painting, even if it is hackwork, is painting: the decoration is here the thing itself. It may be required less for its aesthetic value than to serve a devotional or other purpose, but that purpose is served by its being a painting; and this seems to me a very important difference. It is also true that 'painting' is a misleading word for Greek vase-decoration. It is rather drawing of a kind, but a kind that does not correspond closely to any use of drawing in the Renaissance: neither its commonest employment as preliminary study nor its occasional adaptation as a finished work of art in itself. This, however, seems to me a less important matter. There is no doubt that the drawing on Attic vases lends itself very well to the recognition of different hands by Morellian methods; and such artists as those to whom Beazley devoted his first two studies, the Kleophrades Painter and the Berlin Painter, and many more, are artists of true worth who can properly be studied for the contribution their work makes to our understanding of the history of Greek art. Work of this quality, however, merges gradually into stereotyped and coarsely applied pot-decoration. There is no place to get a knife in; and the method can be legitimately applied across the board, but its application to the lower depths has little to do with the history of fine art.

I feel that at first Beazley did not recognise this ambiguity, or at least did not regard it as important, and perhaps even later only recognised it in a limited degree; and I do think it important that we his followers should. Some change of attitude is implied in his dropping of the word 'Master' and in the absorption of the Berlin Painter's school-pieces into the painter's own oeuvre, or most of them; but when he writes of Group E[16] as 'the soil from which the art of Exekias springs, the tradition which, on his way from fine craftsman to true artist, he absorbs and transcends', he seems to me to over-simplify. The finest of Greek vase-painters, even at his finest, is still at the same time always a worker in a utilitarian craft. I do think we need to spell this ambiguity out. To try to solve the problem by restricting the method to works of good quality is simply to create an artificial and unreal imitation of the conditions prevailing in the study of Italian painting but which do not prevail here. One of the splendid things about Beazley's work is, it seems to me, the steadfast devotion with which he did apply his method to the whole field of Attic vase-painting, regardless of quality. No, that is wrong. He always regarded quality, but he applied his method to everything, good and bad alike, and it was by doing that that he made such a vast difference to our understanding of the subject. For that reason one other attack on his methods seems unnecessary and a pity.

In 1975 Philippe Bruneau published a very interesting and valuable article called 'Situation méthodologique de l'histoire de l'art antique'.[17] He is not primarily concerned with vase-painting, or rather he is concerned with it only in a much wider context. His theme is the use of the terms 'archaeology' and 'art history' and the confusions of thought and method which underlie their confused application to ancient art. He makes a strong plea for the application of rigorous art-historical method to all fields of ancient art, together with the absolute abnegation of any aesthetic value judgements; since such judgements, he holds, are totally subjective. Beazley's treatment of the lower depths of Attic red-figure and black-figure should, I would have thought, fit well into this programme; but he turns aside to attack the whole idea of attributing anonymous works to individual painters on stylistic considerations. He has two main arguments. First, the assumption that no two artists can produce indistinguishable work is false: it is hard, for instance (he says), to know by style the work of Frans Hals from that of his pupil Judith Leysten; how much harder then to be sure that everything one gives to a hypothetical Villa Giulia Painter is really one man's. Secondly, any characteristics which link different works so closely as to allow them to be confidently attributed to one artist are by their nature so limiting that they can only give us a tiny facet of an artist's personality; any artist of any worth produces work too varied to allow him to be reconstituted in this way.

I see some force in these arguments, but not much. What historian of Renaissance painting would claim that a list he gave of an artist's work contained nothing that that artist did not paint and everything which survives that he did? Yet such a list can give a fundamentally true picture of the artist's character and development; and I believe the same is true in the field of Attic vase-painting. Bruneau's objections are extremely theoretical; and I get the feeling, with Bruneau and with Vickers, that they are so in love with theory that they sometimes forget to look back at the objects. I find it really hard to see how, if they look at the works attributed to the Kleophrades Painter, the Berlin Painter, the Pan Painter (to avoid mentioning any whose names we think we know), they could fail to recognise these as real artistic personalities with considerable range and development. They are also, to my eyes, *good* artists, and this seems to me important. Bruneau is of course right that aesthetic judgements are subjective and personal. Indeed value judgements in any field tend now to be rather suspect, and though some of the reasons for this are rather suspect themselves, I think, others are undeniably sound. Such judgements *are* personal, subjective and variable, and so very difficult to apply in any controlled way. Nevertheless, the making of value judgements seems to me an essential part of being human, and to avoid expressing them and so pretend they are not there is a falsification as well as a cowardly course. And then it makes the subject so boring. Some Edwardian lady is recorded as saying that being kissed by a man without a moustache is like eating an egg without salt; and value judgements are to me the salt in art history. I should not be interested in the history of Greek art if I did not think that it is a great artistic tradition, and that while some of it is good some of it is not, and that to make and justify that distinction is part of my business.

That is one aspect of art history. Another, of course, is as part of the whole history of culture and manners, part of sociology and anthropology. If Vickers can show that the rich and aristocratic in Athens used only gold and silver and never looked at a painted vase, that is a matter of great interest, and the question of who did use the painted pottery, the very fine and the hack work, is also very interesting. In the nearly total loss of fine figured silver and gold ware, however, we cannot say a great deal about it as art. The best clay vases are here in quantity and *are* important as works of art in their own right; and also, since their decoration is a kind of drawing, even if they were copied from metal designs they would still tell us more than anything else we have about the development of Greek painting at this stage. Under this sociological aspect Carl Fabergé is no doubt a significant figure; as significant perhaps as his near contemporary Claude Monet, but not as an artist. If an Easter egg by Fabergé fetches as much as a landscape by Monet, that tells us something about the market but nothing about art.

Beazley's work helps us to use Attic pottery for both ends. The great painters at their best are part of the history of fine art in Greece; the rest—and the great painters too of course, at their best as at their worst—part of the pottery business, part of the organisation of Athenian life. There is no sharp distinction. The great painters (the Berlin Painter is a striking example) produced a great deal of mass-produced, aesthetically negligible stuff; and a hack like the Nikosthenes Painter could on his day turn out a masterpiece. Beazley was well enough aware of the differences in quality, as when he wrote of the Nikoxenos Painter in 1914 'but Euthymides is an excellent artist, and our master, to speak truly a clown';[18] and in the later lists there are many much worse artists than the Nikoxenos Painter, as those of whom he wrote in *ARV*[2] (753) 'in dealing with these trifling objects, not the most delightful of one's tasks', or 'the heart-breaking end of the Attic cup'.[19] Now, if a vase can secure an attribution to the Nikoxenos Painter it will probably fetch more money than a better piece for which one cannot find a name. That is a matter for the art market. For academic purposes we do need, I think, to be very sensitive to the distinctions of quality in this ambiguous craft and art of Attic vase-painting. If one of us were to set a student—as God forbid anyone should, but it might happen—to distinguish hands in the F. B. Group, it would be important to remember (and to reassure the victim) that the task would have nothing to do with the history of art but could only be of interest for the statistical light it might throw on the organisation of the Attic pottery business.

One more point. I have talked about Beazley almost exclusively as the attributor of Attic vases; because that was his great work, whether one believes in its validity or not, and whether, believing, one approves of it or not as an approach to the subject. Beazley, however, was not, as we all know, just an attributor. He was a great scholar with a very wide range of deep knowledge in classical art as a whole, and in classical literature too, and in art and literature outside that. We need to remember this, not only in appreciation of Beazley but in regulating our own approach to the subject. When critics suggest that, in Beazley's wake, we are inclined to trivialise our study by assuming that the most interesting thing about a vase is necessarily who painted it; or devote our time, or cause our students to devote their time, to investigating the development of artists of little intrinsic quality, I sometimes feel that they have more of a point than in the broader attacks on Beazley's method which I have been considering. We would do well not to shut our ears to them; but the range and depth of the papers I have heard during the Centenary Colloquia encourages me greatly.

NOTES

1   *JHS* 105 (1985).
2   See Beazley in *AJA* 47 (1943) 456 – 57.
3   *POxy* 52 (1984) 3659, 5 – 8.
4   Athens, Agora, AP 1044. *Hesp* 6 (1937) 468 – 86. *ABV* 145.19.
5   *ARV*² 205 – 206, nos. 123 – 26.
6   *ARV*² 1390.1 – 5; D.C. Kurtz, *Athenian White Lekythoi* (Oxford, 1975) 68 – 73.
7   Eleusis, Museum. Robertson, *Greek Painting* 42, 45.
8   *ABV* 3 – 7, 679. *Para* 1 – 6. *BAdd* 1.
9   London, British Museum, D 2. Robertson, *Greek Painting* (1959) 113. *ARV*² 862.22.
10 Harrow School, 55. *JHS* 30 (1910) pl. 7. *ARV*² 183.11.
11 Würzburg, University, 507. *CVA* ii, pls. 8 – 11. *ARV*² 181.1. On all these see P.E. Corbett, 'Preliminary sketches in Greek vase-painting', in *JHS* 85 (1965) 16 – 28.
12 K.P. Stähler, *Eine unbekannte Pelike des Eucharidesmalers* (Köln/Graz, 1967).
13 Florence, Museo Archeologico, 4209. *ABV* 76.1. Most readily available in *Bollettino d'Arte*, Serie speciale 1, *Vaso François* (1980) 65 – 83 (esp. 82).
14 *OPA* 3 (1985) 237 – 50 (Kurtz).
15 *JHS* 31 (1911) 276 – 95.
16 *BSA* 32 (1934) 3 – 4.
17 *L'antiquité classique* 44 (1975) 425 – 87 (esp. 448 – 51).
18 *BSA* 19 (1914) 247.
19 *ARV*² 753.1406.

BEAZLEY AND SOUTH ITALIAN VASE PAINTING

Dale Trendall

LA TROBE UNIVERSITY, MELBOURNE

DIETRICH VON BOTHMER in his 'Observations on the subject matter of South Italian Vases', a lecture given in the Museum of Fine Arts, Richmond, Virginia, in May 1982, on the occasion of the exhibition held there of vases from Magna Graecia, noted that 'art historians have not always been kind when dealing with South Italian ceramic products' and that 'Beazley himself was rather harsh in the few lines he devoted in *Greek Sculpture and Painting* to the not inconsiderable output'. Beazley's own words, originally written for the chapter on the art of the fourth century for volume six of the *Cambridge Ancient History* are:

> Attic vase-painting touches bottom in the early part of the fourth century ... in the second quarter ... a revival begins. In the Kerch vases—as these latest of Attic red-figure vases are often called—there are flickers of beauty. The tall, dignified figures are a relief from the debased rolypolies of the sub-Meidian period; but they in their turn are often vacuous and mannered, and with its predilection for three-quartered faces and three-quartered and frontal figures, and its neglect of the speaking contour, the style is not really suitable to vase-painting.
>
> In Italy the prospect is not much more pleasing. Some of the phlyax vases, with their scenes from farces, are delightful. The Dolon in London, which may be dated about 400, is not a farce, but a burlesque of epic; in its pattern of men and trees, it is worthy to set beside Pollaiuolo's Battle of the Nudes; in its mastery of the comic, beside the Heracles and Busiris of the old Ionian. When we turn to the big Apulian vases of the second half of the century, we note the slickness of hand and we can put up with a square inch or so here and there; but it is really time that vase-painting ceased; and practically, it ceases, in Italy as well as in Attica, at the end of the century.

As Bothmer goes on to say, this appraisal sounds rather discouraging and one might well have thought in consequence that Beazley had devoted little time and less thought to the problems of South Italian pottery. This is in fact far from the case and although he produced no major works on the subject, his contributions to it are extensive, illuminating and far-reaching, although many of them have to be sought in reviews and footnotes.

31

Early South Italian

In a review of Leroux's catalogue of the Greek vases in the Archaeological
Museum in Madrid (*JHS* 33 (1913) 142 — 43) Beazley gives no specific consideration to the South Italian vases, although they are numerous and many had been
incorrectly classified, quite a number of Early South Italian being listed as Attic.
We may therefore assume that up to this time he had not devoted much attention
to the origins of South Italian. It is, however, clear that ten years later this was
certainly not the case, since Tillyard, in the Introduction to *The Hope Vases* (1923)
10, refers to Beazley's list of Early South Italian vases, of which he had kindly
allowed Tillyard to make use. It was Furtwängler, some twenty-five years earlier,
who had first showed that certain vases previously thought to be Attic were in fact
more probably of local South Italian origin, and it seems highly likely that by
1923 Beazley had already devoted a considerable amount of thought to this very
important group. That he held Furtwängler's work in high esteem may be
deduced from his comment in a review of the first Belgian fascicule of the *CVA*
(*JHS* 46 (1926) 293) to the effect that Furtwängler's '1886 classification of the
Italiote vases in Berlin is still far beyond most museums'.

From the start Beazley was highly critical of the terms 'Greco-Italiote' and
'Attico-Italiote' as applied to Early South Italian vases; in his review (*JHS* 48
(1928) 126) of *CVA*, France 6 (Mouret Collection) he refers to two Attic vases
which the author had called 'Greco-Italiote'—'not a nice word'—and in a
subsequent review of *CVA*, Louvre 5, published in the same year (*JHS* 48 (1928)
270), he notes that 'the word Greco-Italiote appears for the second time—and will
be a comfort to two large classes of people, the lovers of compromise and the lovers
of solecisms'. He adds that 'M. Pottier says it is often difficult to distinguish Attic
vases from Italiote. I think he exaggerates: the two fabrics are frequently
confounded, but unreasonably, for there can seldom be any doubt.'

Beazley then proceeds to list a number of vases ranked as Attic, which are in fact
Early South Italian, and to classify them according to various stylistic groups:

(i) Vases belonging to an Early Italiote group discussed by Tillyard and
himself in *The Hope Vases* (9 — 10). These belong to what is now identified as the
workshop of the Pisticci, Cyclops and Amykos Painters and include such vases as
Louvre G 489, G 498, G 499, G 500, and G 495, to which Beazley added the pelikai
G 542, G 544 and G 552 and the hydriai G 554 and G 555 (not published in the
CVA, but previously taken as Attic);

(ii) Vases associated with the Sisyphus vase in Munich (see *Greek Vases in
Poland*, 72), like Louvre G 493 and G 570;

(iii) The bell-krater G 494, which belongs to the group of the London Dolon
krater.

These groupings add a few more vases to the preliminary classification of Early
South Italian which Beazley makes in *Greek Vases in Poland* (1928, 72 — 4, note 4),
arising out of his description and discussion of the volute-krater (now in Warsaw)
showing 'Peleus struggling with Thetis on the sea-shore', which he points out

'belongs to a group which includes most of the masterpieces of Italiote vase-painting' and adds that 'this group ... leads on through what might be called a Lucano-Apulian phase to the so-called "Apulian" style of the Darius vase and all that, large or small, clusters round it. The difference between our vase and the Darius krater is enormous: but it is the result of time and the changes which time and personalities bring: the succession is unbroken.'

Beazley then listed two other volute-kraters by the same hand as the Peleus and Thetis krater, one in Ruvo (1096) with the rape of the Leucippidae, the other in Munich (3268) with the marriage of Sisyphus, after which he named the artist the Sisyphus Painter. Some twenty other vases are listed as being by this artist or closely akin to his work, and to the list should be added the Oxford fragment with Daedalus and Icarus, which he discussed in detail in *JHS* 47 (1927) 226–30, and there grouped it with the volute-kraters just referred to. His list provided the basis for an extended study of this painter and his associates (like the Painter of the Berlin Dancing Girl) by his pupil Noël Moon (later Mrs Walter Oakeshott), who published her fundamental article 'Some Early South Italian Vase-painters' in 1929 (*BSR* 11, 30–49). Beazley went on to a consideration of the immediate successors of the Sisyphus Painter, referring to the Birth of Dionysos krater in Taranto (8264), the Amazonomachy krater in Brussels (A 1018) and the Sacrifice to Dionysos krater in Naples (2411) as among the more monumental examples of their work (= *RVAp* I, 35, nos. 2/6, 9 and 8), and to four bell-kraters of less elaborate style by an artist whom Noël Moon later named the Tarporley Painter, after the vase in the Marshall Brooks collection in Tarporley (now in the Los Angeles County Museum, 50.8.29 = *RVAp* I, 47, no. 3/10). He then briefly traced the line of descent from the Sisyphean Group to the Darius vase. After that he added a brief account of some of the more significant vases associated with the Dolon krater in the British Museum.

By the end of 1928, therefore, it is clear that Beazley had laid down with some precision the main lines upon which the first South Italian vases had developed in the late fifth and early fourth centuries B.C., and had already identified several of the principal artists, although not all of them had yet been named. As I have already pointed out, Noël Moon carried this work, with Beazley's help and under his direction, a step further in her article 'Some Early South Italian Vase-painters', where specific names are now given to several of the artists, the early Lucanian and Apulian styles more clearly distinguished, and the development of the latter taken down to the work of the Iliupersis Painter in the second quarter of the fourth century.

Before we leave *Greek Vases in Poland*, we may note in passing Beazley's rejection of the term 'Saticulan' which had been used to describe a rather heterogeneous group of vases, some of which had been found at S. Agata dei Goti, the ancient Saticula, and had therefore suggested to Patroni, and even more strongly to Macchioro, that it was probably the site of a local fabric. Tillyard had already shown that most of the so-called Saticulan vases were in fact Attic of the early fourth century, but thought it likely that a small local Campanian fabric might have existed there; Beazley, while not absolutely denying the existence of such a fabric, notes that 'nine-tenths of the vases classed as Saticulan are Attic of that deplorable period, the early fourth century, and that the remaining tenth consists of odds and ends'. The bell-krater, which prompted his observation (Goluchow 35 = Warsaw 142265; *CVA*, Poland 1, pl. 51, 1), seemed to him at the time Italiote, presumably Campanian, rather than Attic, but in his study of Campanian in *JHS* 53 (1943) 70, he inclines to call it Attic rather than Campanian, and I think that today everyone would agree with him in so doing.

The review of the first fascicule of the *CVA* for Lecce (*JHS* 49 (1929) 110), which publishes a good deal of the Early South Italian in that Museum, occasioned further additions to the lists already quoted. Beazley starts off by saying that 'one is glad to see that Italiote is distinguished from Attic, not jumbled up with it, as in other sections of the *Corpus*'. He goes on to make the important observation that 'Italiote red-figure was not exported to Greece and South Russia. There are some Italiote vases in the Athens Museum (e.g. 1422, in the Amykos Group)—but not from Greek sites.' He adds that 'the only place where Dr. Romanelli appears to go astray is in the four vases III Ic, Pls. 7 and 9: these are rightly grouped with Attic in the plates, but in the text they are called Italiote and ascribed to Attic artists working in Italy. As a matter of fact they are pure Attic, made in Athens.' He then deals in some detail with the Early South Italian, noting several vases on pl. 5,3 and 4 to pl. 8 as belonging to the Pisticci—Amykos Group, and on pls. 1 to 5,1 — 2 as by followers or imitators of the Sisyphus Painter (Painter of the Berlin Dancing Girl; Hearst Painter). In his review, two years later (*JHS* 51 (1931) 120), of the second Lecce fascicule, which he calls 'an austere, but uncommonly useful, instalment of the *Corpus* devoted to South Italian vases, most of them Apulian of the Darius class', he notes two connected groups, each consisting of five bell-kraters, which were subsequently identified as the work of the Lecce and Hoppin Painters. He also noted that a few Attic vases had crept in, as well as one Early Lucanian (Creusa Painter) and one Paestan.

It is obvious, then, that by the early 1930's Beazley had formed a clear picture of the origins and development of South Italian in the later fifth and early fourth centuries and had recognized the existence of two main schools of vase-painters, one which led on from the Sisyphus Painter to the developed Apulian style of the Darius Painter and his followers, the other, which began with the Pisticci— Amykos Group, continued in the work of the Dolon and Creusa Painters, and led on to the developed Lucanian style. Apart from passing observations in later reviews, where misattributions are corrected, he does not elaborate further upon what he had already laid down concerning Early South Italian, although his article in *AJA* 56 (1952) 193 — 95 on the New York phlyax vase by the Tarporley Painter sheds new light on both the inscriptions and the subject-matter of this vase, as well as again illustrating his approval of this particular class of Italiote vases.

We may now turn to look at his contribution to later South Italian, in the period when Early South Italian had become more positively Apulian and Lucanian, and when the other regional fabrics, Campanian, Paestan and Sicilian are more clearly defined.

Later Apulian

Later Apulian vase-painting found little favour in Beazley's eyes. He notes in passing the charm of the drawing on the Judgement of Paris epichysis, formerly in the Castle Ashby collection (= *RVAp* I, 428, no. 16/69), but speaks slightingly of 'the general slickness of the work of the Darius Painter and his followers and of the perpetual elegance of late Apulian with its talent for trivialising even the noblest themes'. He sought a suitable term to denote Apulian vases of this style and suggested 'A.P.', standing for Apulian 'pure' or 'Persians'; we felt that perhaps 'Ornate' was more appropriate, since, as Beazley himself pointed out, this style goes back to a much earlier phase of Apulian than the 'Persians' period and has its roots in the work of the Felton, Iliupersis and Lycurgus Painters in the second quarter of the fourth century. Of the very latest Apulian, Beazley mentions the abject quality of such vases as the Lasimos krater in the Louvre or the Cawdor krater in the Soane Museum (*RVAp* II, 914, no. 28/36 and 931, no. 28/119), only to point out that the Icarus krater in Naples (1767) is even worse—an incompetent and hideous imitation. Such strictures are not out of place, since these vases (together with a number of less pretentious pieces) represent the dying gasp of Apulian and their quality was seldom improved by the heavy hand of the 19th century restorer. Since Beazley's day, however, a quite remarkable number of Late Apulian vases has come to light, especially by the Underworld, Baltimore, Arpi and White Saccos Painters, and these have given us a much better understanding of the later phases of this fabric, as well as providing us with many notable and often unique illustrations of Greek mythology and drama.

Lucanian

The two chief later Lucanian vase-painters were identified by Beazley in the 1930's. His unofficial names for them were (i) the Slaver (who later became the Choephoroi Painter), after the slave, holding a strigil and aryballos, who stands behind the man seated on a traveller's pack on the Choephoroi hydria in Munich (= *LCS* 120, no. 602), and (ii) the Birder (later the Primato Painter), from his fondness for depicting birds, especially perched on the fingers of youths or women. Of the former's works no list is given, although, in his review of the second Brussels fascicule of the *CVA* (*JHS* 59 (1939) 149), Beazley attributes the nestoris (R 407) with Orestes and Electra to his hand, associating it with the Munich hydria. Of the latter's work a fairly complete list, containing some fifty vases, is given in his article 'Prometheus Fire-lighter' (*AJA* 43 (1939) 633, note 3) where the artist is now named the Primato Painter, after a somewhat obscure Italian periodical, the 'Primato artistico italiano', in which in 1920 a couple of his vases had been published, and it was pointed out that his style was derived from Apulian vases of the stage just preceding the Darius krater (i.e. the work of the Lycurgus Painter).

Here I may be permitted to diverge for a moment to recount a hitherto unexplained, but amusing, episode in this painter's history. In 1937, D. M. Robinson, when preparing the third fascicule of his vase-collection for the *CVA*, consulted me about a kernos of curious shape by this painter, which consisted of three small lebes-like vases joined to a looped handle and decorated respectively with a bird, the head of a woman and the head of a bearded man. I told him that it was by a Lucanian painter, to whom Beazley referred as the 'Birder', and in the *CVA* he was given the somewhat pretentious name of the Philornithic Painter or Birdmaster, which fortunately soon after gave way to the Primato Painter, a name which still perhaps does him more than justice.

Paestan

It was Patroni (*Ceramica antica nell' Italia meridionale* (1897) 37−79) who first recognized the independent existence of a Paestan fabric. He devoted a substantial section of his work to a discussion of the vases signed by Asteas and Python, and to these he added a number of other vases which he considered to belong to the same style or to represent a development from it, thus establishing a basic nucleus of Paestan vases. Their identification as Paestan met with a certain scepticism; Leroux in his catalogue of the Madrid vases preferred to consider Paestan as a branch of Campanian, and Giglioli in 1925, on the evidence of the Villa Giulia phlyax fragment, saw Taranto as a more likely centre of production. Beazley, in his review of the third fascicule of the Villa Giulia *CVA* (*JHS* 48 (1928) 257) in which Rizzo republished the fragment, notes that 'the Asteas is called Lucanian: the group of vases which clusters round the signed vases of Asteas and Python is so homogeneous and distinctive that we should do well to keep calling it Paestan—as a conventional name—even if it is not certainly by Poseidonians'. Subsequent excavations, which have brought to light almost a thousand Paestan vases from the various cemeteries around the city, have removed any lingering doubts about the correct designation of the fabric.

It is, however, in his article on the Paestan bell-krater acquired by the Ashmolean Museum in 1942 (*AJA* 48 (1944) 357−66) that Beazley makes his most substantial contribution to the study of Paestan pottery. He compares the Oxford krater with one formerly in the Disney collection and now in Cambridge (GR 7. 1943), and uses them as a basis for an illuminating comparison of the styles of Asteas and Python, pointing out that the two must have worked together and that the technique, composition, patternwork, and drawing of the figures are so alike that the hypothesis of two neighbouring establishments, influencing each other, is less probable than that of a single establishment: the workshop of Asteas and Python. In the past forty years a great many new vases from this workshop have come to light; they entirely confirm Beazley's judgement, and show that the Oxford and Cambridge kraters come from what is now quite a large group of very similarly decorated kraters, nearer in style to Python than to Asteas, and in all probability early work of the former.

Beazley goes on to stigmatize the more pretentious products of this workshop as failures—the signed Alcmena by Python and his Orestes at Delphi (= British Museum F 149 and 1917.12−10.1 = *Paestan Pottery*, pls. 15 and 17); the Kadmos and Hesperides by Asteas (Naples 3226 and 2873 = *PP*, pl. 5a and pl. 4); he sees more merit in some of the phlyax vases, and in the many two-figure compositions, in which he finds the 'agreeable tang of popular, provincial art'.

His assessment might well be described as 'severe but just' and the great wealth of new material merely confirms his acute perception.

Campanian

Of all the South Italian fabrics, it is to Campanian that Beazley made the most significant contribution. His fundamental study 'Groups of Campanian Red-figure' (*JHS* 63 (1943) 66−111) marked an enormous step forward in our knowledge of that fabric and provided a solid foundation for all future studies of it. When one reflects that it was put together during the war years when, as Beazley records, the accessible material was comparatively scanty—'poor or incomplete published reproductions, a few photographs, a few originals, and not many notes'—it is an immense tribute to his genius that he was able to put together the framework of a very thorough classification of the fabric and that, although it has subsequently been possible substantially to increase the lists of attributed vases and add some new painters, virtually no other changes were called for.

We may begin with the Owl-Pillar Group which Beazley first put together in *Greek Vases in Poland*, noting that the group consisted largely of neck-amphorae, which, in semi-barbarous style, imitate Attic originals of the second and third quarters of the fifth century, and are decorated with large figures, marvellously crude. Beazley saw that they had no connection with Campanian vase-painting of the fourth century, but thought that the available evidence, especially of their finding places, pointed to their having been made in Campania. More recently Dr Hadzisteliou-Price (*ArchEph* 1974, 168−98) has seen in them descendants of the Campanian black-figure style, but the connection seems to me rather tenuous, though perhaps sufficient to confirm the likely Campanian origin of these curious vases.

Campanian proper Beazley divides into several groups—an earlier one which includes the Cassandra and Parrish Painters, with their immediate followers, as well as the Capua Painter, a forerunner of the slightly later AV Group, which contains some of the most characteristic Campanian vases, especially those of the Libation and Danaid Painters. He then looks briefly at the Caivano Painter and cognates, vases which I had originally thought of as Paestan, since many came from that site, but which I would now think of rather as Campanian, with a strong Paestan affinity. Thereafter Beazley turns to a large group of vases many of which were found at Cumae and, although he does not definitely commit himself to their being Cumaean, he feels that this is a probability; he identifies the CA and (Boston) Ready Painters, and the Painter of New York GR 1000, going on to discuss the later vases of the Apulianizing phase and especially the work of the APZ Painter, which, as he rightly points out, must have been produced in the same city and even in the same workshop as those of the CA Painter, but which are in style almost pure Apulian. He puts forward the theory that these vases were most likely to be the work of an 'Apulian' painter who established himself in Campania, rather than Campanian imitations of Apulian, and this is confirmed by the contemporary work of the Aphrodite Painter at Paestum (not then come to light), who brought an Apulian style to that fabric, and was later followed by other Apulianizers. Beazley's identification of the Apulianizing phase in Campanian marked a great advance in our understanding of South Italian stylistic connections. He then turns to some of the later Campanian artists, notably the Ixion Painter, who drew to a greater extent on mythology for his subjects than was usual in Campanian, and to the later descendants of the AV Group and of the Cumaeans, concluding with the almost completely barbarized painters.

In the circumstances, it was a masterly survey of the fabric and its relations with Apulian and Paestan, and it placed large numbers of vases, the correct classifications of which had previously been a matter of dispute or uncertainty, firmly in their proper place.

Sicilian

In the course of his study of Campanian he referred to a few vases which stood somewhat apart from the others, notably the Lloyd krater in Oxford, and three round pyxides connected by shape and decoration, with ivy on the lids and female heads on the bowls. The last he thought might even have found a place in his Group H, which he calls Sicilian(?). He begins this group with two large skyphoid pyxides, one formerly in the collection of Borelli Bey and now in that of Mrs Randolph Hearst at Hillsborough, the other in Palermo, adding in a footnote a list of 'Campanian' vases of this shape, which include many that would now be regarded as Sicilian, such as Moscow 510 and 505 (the missing Canfarelli vase), and which he discusses in the light of several other vases of somewhat similar style and of Sicilian provenience. Beazley notes that this might be chance, but that the possibility they were also made there is not to be dismissed and that a Sicilian fabric should have points of contact with Campanian would be natural enough. He refers to Pace's support for the Sicilian origin of such vases, but modestly adds that he cannot contribute anything new to the controversy. The excavations at Lipari, Lentini, Gela and other Sicilian sites during the past forty years have shown that he was entirely correct in his suggestions and a true Sicilian red-figure fabric has now emerged, to which all the vases mentioned by Beazley are now clearly seen to belong. It is a convincing demonstration of his skill in seeing both stylistic affinities and differences.

Non-Red-Figured Vases

(i) WITH SUPERPOSED COLOUR

In *Etruscan Vase-painting* (218 – 29) Beazley devotes a particularly useful section to certain groups of Italiote vases in the added-colour technique, as these have sometimes been confused with Etruscan and are not always easy to distinguish. Among the more important of the vases decorated in added colour are the Xenon Group of Apulian, from the later fifth century onwards, which consists mainly of kantharoids and kantharoi imitating Attic of the St. Valentin class, and oenochoai

of various shapes, decorated with scroll, wave, meanders, laurel etc.; there are also Campanian imitations of the St. Valentin skyphoi, mostly from Cumae and Capua. Apulian are the vases, almost always stemless cups, of the Red Swan Group, decorated in the interior with a swan or some other creature in added red, or with a palmette-fan, sometimes painted on top of an impressed design. There are a few Campanian vases with figured designs in added colour (e.g. the late Spectre Group), and many more may be classified as Paestan, mostly from the workshop of Asteas and Python, but some from the later groups. To Beazley must go the credit for the first reasonably complete analysis and classification of these various groups of vases decorated with applied red.

(ii) KEMAIS

A further group of Campanian vases, recognized by Patroni and studied more closely by Gabrici, is what Beazley calls the Kemai Group, deriving its name from the first line of the long inscription painted on British Museum F 507. They are connected with the late Campanian red-figured vases from Teano, and one is actually decorated with a female head in red-figure, though on the few others which bear figured designs, they are usually in black outline. Most of them are small stamnoid-vessels with a lid, decorated with black pattern-work on a reserved ground or white on black. Beazley lists 36 such vases; the list was greatly expanded by Mingazzini (Capua, *CVA* 3, IV Es) and the total now runs to some 200.

(iii) BLACK WARE

Beazley also drew attention firmly to the fact that Campania does not have a monopoly of black vases with impressed decoration, pointing out rather sternly in his review of the Sèvres *CVA* (*JHS* 56 (1936) 252 – 54) that 'though it seems still to be thought that this is indeed the case, such vases were an Attic invention and appear in Greece from the second half of the fifth century onwards.'

(iv) GNATHIA

Of Gnathia little is said, but in a review of the first British Museum fascicule of the *CVA* (*JHS* 45 (1925) 286), which contained a section on Gnathia, he points out that it fails to distinguish what may be called 'Gnathia' proper—a late Apulian ware—from very different fabrics, such as Campanian, and even a bowl (F 542) from the Hesse Group, perhaps made, like the Pocola, in Latium.

Etruscan

So far we have looked only at Beazley's contribution to South Italian, which, if to a great extent sporadic, yet none the less left an abiding mark upon the subject and provided solid foundations on which other scholars were able to build. He outlined the map of South Italian with a sure hand and, if it has fallen to others to chart the individual territories in greater detail, it was never necessary for them to change the boundaries or relocate the principal centres of manufacture. This is surely no mean achievement on the part of one who did not pretend to make a detailed study of the whole field.

Lastly, I turn briefly to Etruscan, the other area of non-Attic pottery to which Beazley made a vital contribution. Here he give us a much more systematic study, firstly in his chapters of the catalogue of *La Raccolta Benedetto Guglielmi nel Museo Gregoriano Etrusco* (1939) and, more importantly, in *Etruscan Vase-painting* (1947). The Guglielmi catalogue, written in collaboration with Filippo Magi who dealt with the non-figured vases and the small bronzes, gives us annotated lists of over sixty black- and red-figure Etruscan vases, as well as those decorated in applied colour or solely in black glaze, and introduces us to the Micali Painter, one of the most prolific of Etruscan black-figure artists, of whose work and that of painters closely associated with him, we are presented with a comprehensive survey. The book, however, remains primarily a catalogue, unlike *Etruscan Vase-painting* where the subject is treated in a very different way. Here, too, classified lists are provided, but individual vases are often discussed in considerable detail, in the course of which fresh light is shed for us not only on Etruscan vase-painting but on a host of other topics as well—bronzes, wall-paintings, mythology, armour and even elephants. As Beazley says in his introduction to the work—it began as a study of Etruscan red-figure, to which appendices were then added on black-figure, vases decorated in applied colours, black vases, etc., thus transforming it into a study of Etruscan vase-painting as a whole and dealing with the subject on a scale never before attempted. He goes on to say that 'the treatment may appear somewhat scrappy in places', and attributes this in part to the derivative character of Etruscan art, which for this reason 'is apt to proceed by fits and starts'. He adds that 'clay vases were not their forte: but even these may help towards the understanding of a people which had some touch of greatness'. As Martin Robertson pointed out in a very perceptive review of the book (*JHS* 69 (1949) 93 − 94), this gives the key to Beazley's treatment of the subject, in which, because of the inferior quality of Etruscan vase-painting, there is less scope for the exercise of his unparalleled sense of styles but by way of compensation we are allowed to share his knowledge and understanding of a far wider range of topics than we might have expected. Beazley expresses the hope that his work will at least lead to many Etruscan vases being brought out of their lurking-places, scrutinized and published and the past thirty years or so have seen this hope triumphantly fulfilled.

Passing mention may also be made of a paper delivered by Beazley in Oxford in 1947 and published in the *JHS* in 1949; it was entitled 'The World of the Etruscan Mirror' and deals with the scenes engraved on a number of bronze mirrors from the sixth to the third centuries B.C. They show a great variety of subject and style and here, as so often elsewhere, Beazley has opened a door which allows us to enter into a new world which he invites us to explore for ourselves, giving us a series of sign-posts to help us on our way. His summing up would serve equally well for South Italian vase-painting: 'There is much repetition, but much that is individual and, in our experience, unique; great difference of quality, but not a little beauty. Where there is no beauty there is at least information to be had.'

Nobody knows better than I do how much every student of South Italian pottery owes to the work, both published and unpublished, of J.D. Beazley, and it gives me the greatest pleasure, on the occasion of his centenary, to pay tribute to a scholar of whom it might be said with complete justice:

Nihil quod tetigit non ornavit.

BIBLIOGRAPHY

I.   SOUTH   ITALIAN

The works listed below deal with, or make passing reference to, South Italian vase-painting:

'Icarus', in *JHS* 47 (1927) 222 – 33.
Greek Vases in Poland (Oxford, 1928) 72 – 77.
'Notes on the Vases in Castle Ashby', in *BSR* 11 (1929) 29.
'Prometheus Fire-lighter', in *AJA* 43 (1939) 633 – 35 (esp. note 3).
'Groups of Campanian Red-figure', in *JHS* 63 (1943) 66 – 111.
'A Paestan Vase', in *AJA* 48 (1944) 357 – 66.
'The New York Phlyax Vase', in *AJA* 56 (1952) 193 – 95.

The following reviews of various fascicules of the *Corpus Vasorum Antiquorum* in the *Journal of Hellenic Studies* make useful comments on, or attributions of, South Italian vases:

Corpus Vasorum Antiquorum	*JHS*
British Museum 1	45 (1925) 286
British Museum 2 ⎫ Brussels 1 ⎭	46 (1926) 291 – 93
U.S.A. 1 (Hoppin and Gallatin Collections)	47 (1927) 148 – 49
France 6 (Collection Mouret)	48 (1928) 126 – 27
Italy 3 (Villa Giulia 3)	48 (1928) 257
France 8 (Louvre 5)	48 (1928) 270 – 71
Italy 4 (Lecce 1)	49 (1929) 110
Italy 6 (Lecce 2)	51 (1931) 120
Poland 1 (Musée Czartoryski)	52 (1932) 142
France 12 (Louvre 8)	53 (1933) 310
Poland 2 (Cracow)	56 (1936) 92 – 93
France 15 (Sèvres)	56 (1936) 252 – 54
Poland 3	56 (1936) 254
Brussels 2	59 (1939) 149
Brussels 3	70 (1950) 88
France 16 (Musée Rodin)	72 (1952) 156

See also the review in *JHS* 54 (1934) 90−92 of Ernst Langlotz, *Martin von Wagner Museum der Universität Würzburg*: *Griechische Vasen*.

II.   ETRUSCAN

With F. Magi, *La Raccolta Benedetto Guglielmo nel Museo Gregoriano Etrusco* (Vatican, 1939). Vol. I − Vasi dipinti greci ed etruschi (Etruschi, nos. 82−143).
Etruscan Vase-painting (Oxford, 1947).
'Etruscan Red-figure in Rome and Florence', in *Annuario* 24−26 (1946−48) 141.
'Gleanings in Etruscan Red-figure', in *Festschrift Andreas Rumpf* (Cologne, 1958) 10−13.

100 YEARS OF CLASSICAL ARCHAEOLOGY IN OXFORD

John Boardman

LINCOLN PROFESSOR

In 1877 a commission on the University of Oxford recommended the creation of new professorships which would deal with subjects not covered by the teaching in colleges. And in the next year a petition was presented to the Hebdomadal Council of the University urging the creation of a museum of archaeology and art which would house the marble statues already in the University's possession, but also that 'most space would naturally be required for the series of casts to illustrate the whole history of Greek and Roman Sculpture' and to what it called 'copies of the chief products of the Industrial Arts of Greece and Rome'. The petition was signed by a hundred and thirty-two professors, tutors of colleges and others interested in university education, and included all the leading classical scholars of the day, with orientalists, philologists, and, for instance, Oscar Wilde. They also subscribed to purchase the nucleus of a Cast Collection in 1884 (the total sum was £630 10s. 6d.).[1] No action was taken to create a professorship until 1884 and the first Professor was appointed in 1885, in the year of Beazley's birth. This bare introduction to my subject conceals much that is peculiar to the way things were done, and are still done, in Oxford, and some explanation is called for.

It is difficult to explain the ways of the University of Oxford even to those who have long worked in and for it. It is almost impossible to explain to the visitor from other universities. I make the attempt, because although Oxford traditionally regards itself as the centre of the World, if not the Universe itself, I who came from outside Oxford, must sympathize with the uninitiated. I shall simplify grossly and start with the present. Most Oxford colleges are long established institutions, some very wealthy, which provide a social and domestic environment for students regardless of their subject. But they also, through their tutors, called fellows, supply personal instruction to the students in all major subjects. The University, in so far as it can be detected as an entity, is responsible for examinations and the award of degrees; it provides museums, libraries and laboratories; and it pays professors, readers and lecturers to teach for the whole University in all subjects. At present the overlap is total; most college tutors or fellows also lecture for the whole University, while University professors also belong to and serve colleges. But you can see how the possibility of conflict might arise, and over one hundred years ago, when the colleges were still dominant and the modern University barely formed, the conflict was more apparent.

Some scholars clamoured for the creation of University professorships so that the University would be seen to be dealing with the full range of scholarship, scholarly teaching and research in a manner comparable with that of other European universities. Others were suspicious and thought it was all far better left to the colleges. Some colleges upheld the highest standards of teaching and research, but there was still a large proportion of college fellows whose attitudes had been formed in the days when, for instance, all college fellows were unmarried and when most were priests.[2] In this atmosphere the creation of a Chair in Classical Archaeology was something of a triumph, and it owes its inception not only to the voices of classical scholars but also to the University's already considerable holdings of relevant material.

The University owned a large part of the great seventeenth-century collection of ancient marbles made by the Earl of Arundel. These statues had languished unloved in various places, mainly in and around the Sheldonian Theatre.[3] But in 1845 the University Galleries were built, a structure we now know as the Ashmolean Museum. The statues and some casts were in due course to be housed there, in the care of the new Professor. They formed part of the Department of Classical Archaeology and remained in the Professor's care until 1925 when the responsibility for the marbles was transferred to the Keeper of the Department of Antiquities in the Ashmolean Museum. This Department was created in the last decade of the nineteenth century, mainly by its first Keeper, Arthur Evans, who brought together into new rooms, built on to the University Galleries, the University's archaeological holdings. The rather surprising partnership of Professor Gardner and Evans were to lay sure foundations on which the study of Classical Archaeology in Oxford could be built. 'Together we reigned', wrote Gardner, 'without any friction or jealousy.'[4] This, of course, is part of another story to which I shall allude later, but it can be seen how the presence of the University Galleries and Ashmolean Museum made possible a home and teaching base for the new Professorship.

The Chair was attached to Lincoln College, a fifteenth-century foundation, situated in the centre of Oxford. Its recently retired Rector, Mark Pattison, had been prominent in the discussion about the desirability of professors, and had eventually decided they were a good thing. The new Rector, Merry, was a classicist, who edited the Odyssey and Aristophanes. And the first Lincoln Professor, William Ramsay, took up his post in 1885. There were problems. Ramsay was not the type of scholar well suited to what Oxford expected of classical archaeology. After little more than a year he left Oxford and went to Aberdeen, where he continued in a distinguished career as a scholar of classical Anatolia. In Oxford there had been no money for him. Difficulties in revising their statutes meant that Lincoln College could not pay its new Professor. In a debate in the House of Lords Archbishop Tait remarked that 'some of these professorships were more ornamental than useful'. So the salary had to be sought from another Oxford college, Merton, and, for many years the Lincoln Chair was called the Lincoln and Merton Chair, although the Professor worked in and for Lincoln College.[5] In 1909 Magdalen College too, for a while, contributed to the professorial stipend, and it was only after 1925 that the University undertook all the professor's salary and the Lincoln Chair became, quite simply, the Lincoln Chair.

The rapid defection of the first Professor called forth no little comment. Arthur Evans had certainly considered whether he wanted the Chair, but there is no evidence that he ever applied for it.[6] But once Ramsay left, Arthur gave voice to his views about Oxford in general and its attitude to classical archaeology in particular in a poem, unpublished, which Anne Brown, of the Department of Antiquities in the Ashmolean Museum, kindly drew to my attention, and which I quote here in full:

> Lines by an Oxford hack on hearing that Mr Ramsay who occupied the Chair of Classical Art and Archaeology in that University, being left without a sufficient income on which to live had resigned the Professorship and accepted the Chair of Humanity at Aberdeen.

> Oxford to glorify her Lapidarium
> Made a Professor, minus honorarium;
> The new Professor finding stones and head
> Were not convertible, discreetly fled.
> What then? Does Oxford lose? Our University
> Has still some comfort left in its adversity
> Learning is good, no doubt, we wish to keep
> Its representatives, but on the cheap.
> These poor Professors, its a shame to ridicule 'em
> Are after all outside our true Curriculum
> Our aim's to join in one well-framed anatomy
> A young man's club and 'finishing Academy'.
> We've only one advice to those we love
> 'Be tutorized, and keep along the groove'
> Tread as a man the beaten paths the boy did,
> Let all Professor's lectures be avoided,
> Research is hugely out of place in College—
> Examination is the goal of knowledge;
> A 'subject' should be finite: every fact
> Be cut and dried and in a text book packed.
> Inscriptions, Explorations, Archaeology
> Are incompatible with true philology.
> A Chair for such upon our course encroaches
> Confounds our primers and upsets our Coaches.
> So having trespassed thus on our urbanity
> Let Ramsay go, and teach the Scots humanity.
> Our business is to cram, we are not fools
> Our capital's invested in the Schools.
> Hellenic Art's not needed for a Class
> And healthy barbarism most benefits a 'pass',

Fat fellowships and fees are Consolation
For those who cater to Examinations.

So a new Professor had to be found, and *was* found in the person of Percy
Gardner, who occupied the Chair from 1887 until his retirement thirty-eight years
later, in 1925, at the age of seventy-two. It was a long and important tenure,
because under Gardner the subject was finally established in the University
curriculum. But it was no easy matter and Gardner has never been given credit for
all he did. 'There were still many members of the University', wrote George Hill,
years later,[7] '... who classed archaeology, which they called playing with
potsherds, along with other useless and undignified pursuits, such as biology,
which meant dissecting rabbits.'

Gardner was thirty-four when he came to Oxford. He came from Cambridge—
a very reputable source, and one travelled by two of his successors in the Lincoln
Chair, Martin Robertson and myself. He had also been a professor in Cambridge
for seven years, in the Disney Chair of Archaeology, which was not specifically
devoted to classical archaeology; and he also occupied a research post in the Coin
Room of the British Museum. He found Lincoln College a 'kindly house' and was
given the rooms once occupied by John Wesley, Founder of the Methodist
movement. He admired Oxford, and the teaching of Literae Humaniores; he
wished he had studied there, though seemed to regret the apparent aim, to fit
candidates for the examination for the Indian Civil Service.

Gardner is not easy to judge. Anecdotes about him, by those who remember
him, or those who remember those who remember him, are generally unkind and
they are also unfair. His reputation suffered in Oxford by comparison with that of
his successor Beazley, who was cast wholly in the Oxford mould. But Gardner was
seventy-two when he retired and should be judged in the terms of the nineteenth
century in which he passed most of his working life, and not of the twentieth.[8]

I shall not dwell on Gardner's scholarship, which is no part of my subject. It was
certainly not of the quality of Beazley's. But it was also far wider ranging that that
of any of his successors, and it did not lack depth, at least in numismatics. His *Types
of Greek Coins* (Cambridge, 1883) is still valuable and we still use his *Numismatic
Guide to Pausanias* (written with F. Imhoof-Blumer 1885—87). It was Percy
Gardner who, with Dr Poole, inaugurated the great series of British Museum
Catalogues of Greek Coins, and wrote most of six of the volumes himself. Gardner
also wrote the first catalogue of Greek vases in the Ashmolean Museum and
published supplements to it.[9] In 1880 he helped to create and started to edit the
Journal of Hellenic Studies. In 1892 his book, *New Chapters in Greek History*, presented
to students and a wider intellectual public a shrewd assessment of the archaeological discoveries of the century, through Schliemann, the excavations on the
Athenian Acropolis and at Olympia, to the work of Petrie, at Naucratis in Egypt.
His brother Ernest, then Director of the British School at Athens, which celebrates
its centenary in 1986, had worked there; and later, Hogarth, another Oxford
figure, was to follow them. Gardner's very nineteenth-century attitude to all this is
well reflected in the opening to his chapter on Naucratis: 'Since the bombardment

of Alexandria by the English fleet, learned excavators, equipped by the Egypt Exploration Fund, have been at work in the Delta.' The bombardment happened in 1882 and heralded fifty years of British colonial rule in Egypt. Gardner was used to history in the making. The essays are not wide-eyed art history, but sturdy accounts of how archaeology was writing and rewriting Greek history. We do not need to read them now, but in their day they showed the way to a broader approach to classical archaeology which was regarded with somewhat less suspicion in Britain than in other European countries, though this suspicion, even in Britain and in Oxford, is by no means dead. But the association betweeen classical archaeology and ancient history in Oxford has ever since been strong and productive.

Throughout Gardner's career he wrote about evolutionary Christianity as well as classical archaeology.[10] This was not, on the whole, a subject which endeared him to Oxford, and his reputation suffered for it. His role in university life was of far greater importance and relevance to us. He gathered into the Ashmolean the University's collection of marbles which he found 'dispersed in all sorts of places, and ... mostly in a miserable condition from dirt and neglect'. He had them cleaned and removed the 'most objectionable of the restorations',[11] many of which have since been put on again. The collection of ancient marbles remained in his care until his retirement. The Ashmolean Keeper of Antiquities purchased statues, but the major acquisitions were made by the Professor. Thus, when the Hope Collection was sold in 1917, Gardner succeeded in buying statues from it by asking colleges to make grants for the purpose. When he considered the University collection of casts he complained, in 1888, that the collection of about a hundred and twenty was 'well selected, but too small to be fairly representative—it is about one-sixth as large as the Cambridge collection, one-third as large as the collection at South Kensington [in the Victoria and Albert Museum], and one-twentieth as large as that at Berlin.' Annually he bullied the University into making him a grant to buy more casts and he relentlessly built up the collection until, on his retirement, it was at least as large as that in Cambridge. And in 1914 he wrote the only published account of the Cast Collection. By this time virtually all the ground floor of the Museum was devoted to the Department of Classical Archaeology, with the marbles in the Randolph Gallery and the casts in the area behind it, which is now occupied by the Department of Eastern Art. All this was a remarkable achievement, but a Department of Classical Archaeology cannot live on marble and plaster alone.

Gardner had also bullied the University into making grants towards the creation of a better library. In the Department of Antiquities Arthur Evans had a small library, and Gardner and Evans made a joint appeal to the University to establish a single library of archaeology and to fund it adequately. This was the birth of the classical archaeological section of the present Ashmolean Library, which by now justly enjoys an international reputation.

He acquired photographs too, including many fine nineteenth-century ones of Greece.[12] This was his contribution to the material of his Department. In teaching, he established a paper on Greek Sculpture for classical undergraduates in the first part of the degree (Moderations, or 'Mods') course and taught special subjects which were allowed in the final examination (Greats), including one on Greek Mythology in relationship to Art. The paper in Greek Sculpture came in 1890 as the result of a passionate appeal in a private pamphlet entitled *Classical Archaeology at Oxford*. In 1907 the Diploma in Classical Archaeology was inaugurated. Among its earliest candidates were a distinguished, but perhaps unlikely pair—Joan Evans, the half-sister of Arthur Evans and a distinguished mediaevalist in later years; and Gordon Childe, who was to become the doyen of British prehistorians. Both were taught by Gardner, both received instruction on Greek vases from the young Beazley, then one of the Students (Fellows) of Christ Church.[13]

Gardner was very proud of his pupils. Throughout his teaching career he kept a carefully indexed record of their work. When he retired he counted 757 men pupils and 129 women, whom he taught personally, and he listed separately what he called the 'more distinguished'. They include a remarkable series of names, and his comments on their progress and quality are enlightening. One of his terms of praise was 'has eyes'—a quality which the classical archaeologist above all requires—but which is today in some places discounted. He was wary of what he called the fanciful or conceited, and in Beazley he detected a special quality, to which I shall return. Here are some of his pupils:

Leonard Woolley, the excavator of Ur;
E. Wilenski, the art historian, who exercised an odd fascination over the young Beazley for some years;
J. G. Milne, who 'spent too much time on the river';
J. N. L. Myres, who 'asked questions';
Stanley Robinson, the great numismatist;
Guy Dickins, who catalogued part of the Acropolis collection;
Forsdyke and Wolfenden, both later Directors of the British Museum;
Woodward, the epigraphist;
Beazley;
Hugh Last, later Professor of Roman History in Oxford;
Bernard Ashmole;
Ian Richmond;
A. H. M. Jones, later Professor of Ancient History at Cambridge;
A. W. Lawrence and Jocelyn Toynbee, both later Professors of Classical Archaeology at Cambridge;
H. R. W. Smith;
R. Collingwood, philosopher and archaeologist;
W. Heurtley, the prehistorian;
H. Stuart-Jones;
G. Wainwright, the Near Eastern archaeologist;
Noël Moon, who was to contribute so much to the study of South Italian vases.

Gardner also made shrewd observations about Oxford's lecturing habits—the hopelessness of announcing lectures for undergraduates at 9 a.m., and among Oxford teachers 'a deficiency of social feeling ... unless they have a definite interest in a paper when announced they seldom come to hear it as a matter of duty.'

Oxford changes little.

He was not, of course, alone in teaching. In early days he had the support of Farnell, who made his name in the study of Greek hero cults, and of John Myres, whose interest lay more in Greek prehistory. Myres went to Liverpool in 1907 but returned to Oxford as the Wykeham Professor of Greek History in 1910. Though the Chair was in history he lectured on the archaeology of the Homeric period, and the peculiarly Oxford term 'Homeric Archaeology' appears first in the lecture list in 1911. From 1920 Miss Lorimer began to take over the lectures from the Professor, and the subject Homeric Archaeology joined Greek Sculpture as a paper for undergraduates. Although Gardner had written enthusiastically about Schliemann's discoveries he, like Beazley, had little sympathy for Greek prehistory. 'I therefore regret', he wrote, 'that there is now a tendency, among University students, to study the prehistoric art of the Aegean rather than historic Greek art. It is of course an immeasureably easier task.'[14]

I have already mentioned Gardner's fight with the University to get money for casts and books. He belonged to the age of the pamphleteer, and there is a number of documents which he published or circulated on various topics—some of general public interest, about education and the role of the classics, some with precise University targets. These could be about the provision of pensions for professors, but were more often devoted to the needs of his subject and the difficulties he found in securing for it a safe place in the Oxford system. In early days they brought out elements of the old college-versus-university friction, but there were other threats to ward off, not least a certain indifference to, or suspicion of, his subject shown by some members of the Faculty. He fought for university posts in Greek and Roman epigraphy, one of which was eventually secured for Marcus Tod. He fought even for the study of architecture in the University, without success. With Myres he wrote about classical archaeology in schools. He was sympathetic to the sciences. In 1933 he wrote:[15]

> Indeed, the teachers of physical science at Oxford have been more sympathetic towards archaeology than those teachers of the classics who have tended to think rather of words than of things, and to esteem elegant expression as more important than right thinking. This prejudice however has tended to disappear ... The lecturers on Greek literature are beginning to see in [archaeology] rather a friend than a rival.

He went on:

> Unfortunately, ... there has arisen a tendency to extreme specialization, to take up some small plot in the wide field, and to cultivate it rather intensively than extensively. The tendency probably originated in the German universities ... here it is more fatal, as English scholars lack the amazing power of application which is shewn by their German colleagues ... The specialist ... is apt, like the spider, to spread his web over a little corner of knowledge, and to regard all who come his way as intruders.

But he was generally respectful of German scholarship: 'Scholars in England have been content, with very few exceptions, to take up and rearrange the results of the labours of continental specialists',[16] though he took issue with Furtwängler over the creation of the Athena Lemnia.[17]

In a fine essay for the *Oxford and Cambridge Review* of 1907 he wrote of 'Oxford's Antiquated Machinery', explaining what he called the 'invertebratedness' of the University and appealing for a better definition of the role of university and colleges. A memorandum to the University Commission appealed for a proper place for the teaching of the history of art in the University, an appeal which ranged beyond Oxford's blindness in this area:

> This obtuseness to our historic surroundings, this failure to train the eyes as well as the intelligence, this neglect of the aesthetic faculties, runs through the whole of English education. The Americans make much of the poor morsels of antiquity which they possess; the French, Germans, Greeks and Italians are very proud of the legacies in architecture and art left them by their ancestors. The English are beyond most peoples indifferent to such remains. And we who dwell in the most beautiful and the most historic of English cities keep the eyes of intelligence and sympathy closed against them.

Elsewhere he returned to the theme of the young:[18]

> Young England, as a rule, is not sensitive to the charms of art: ... Most of my pupils have come from the public schools: and however excellent be, in some respects, the training given by those schools, boys leave them with a very rudimentary development of the particular faculties to which I have to appeal, namely, love of the beautiful and intellectual curiosity. Nor do the games such as cricket tend, as one might have fancied, to educate the eye to that keen perception of detail which is of untold value throughout life: on the contrary, I have found that youths, unless they have had some training in physical science, or done field work of some kind, are less exact and discriminating in their observation than girls of the same age.

He nevertheless opposed the entry of women to the University in 1896, and never changed his views about this, though he taught many. That women could for so long be *in* the University but not *of* it is another Oxford peculiarity.

He often reverted to the problems of the relationship of his subject to the more traditional study of Classics:[19]

> Archaeology is well content to be the servant of history, but she will never consent to becoming the handmaid of literature. Nothing in the whole progress of archaeology has so much tended to dwarf and retard the study as the literary prepossessions of those who have taken it up with a view merely to the purposes of commentators, in order to explain difficult passages in the Greek and Roman writers. Many passages can be explained only by archaeology, but that is most distinctly not the purpose for which archaeology should be taken up. ... it is impossible, absolutely impossible, for a University which teaches ancient history scientifically, to continue long deaf to the claims of archaeology.

Beazley succeeded Gardner in 1925 and remained Professor until his retirement in 1956 — 31 years in office to Gardner's 38. His status and role as a scholar of genius are no part of my subject. The contrast with Gardner must have been dramatic. Gardner—patriarchal, a figure of the nineteenth century, a pioneer and empire builder. Beazley—the aesthete, poet (stronger in imagery than finish, and although his friend the poet and playwright, James Elroy Flecker, complained that Beazley had abandoned poetry, I think it was probably a good thing), and with a total dedication mainly to one branch of classical archaeology, though with a far reaching competence in classics.[20] Under Beazley the rapid growth of the Cast Gallery ceased, and the Marbles had been handed over to the care of the Department of Antiquities. Nor, surprisingly, was there any extension of undergraduate teaching into his own chosen subject of Greek vases. Gardner had noted Beazley's excellence as a pupil, but also detected fastidiousness.[21] The fastidious, in the *Oxford Dictionary*, are carefully selective and hard to please. Beazley's generosity to those working on his subject was total, but his was not the temperament to fight for it. I have found one paper in which he expresses anxiety that there was no proper provision in his Department for photographs, though he noted with pleasure that the Library was excellent, and the 'Casts probably on the whole the best in the country'. But he was not able to stop the Library taking rooms from the Cast Gallery to house ancient history. It is not possible to imagine from his pen a diatribe like Gardner's great paper on *Oxford's Antiquated Machinery* or *Oxford at the Cross Roads*. But it was Beazley who compiled the complete catalogue of the casts, noting carefully which noses, arms or ears were original, which not, and providing a detailed bibliography. Beazley too saw to it that the Ashmolean collection of vases continued to grow to be the fine and representative teaching collection it now is and he wrote the labels for them in the austere manner which the Department is only now gradually abandoning. He too ensured the continuing excellence of the Library.

The next major advance came with his successor and friend, Bernard Ashmole, who was persuaded into the Chair in 1956, and held it for just five years. Ashmole came from a Chair at the University of London, and before that the British Museum, a path trodden also by his successor, Martin Robertson. Under Ashmole Greek Vases was at last established as an undergraduate subject with a paper in Mods. Moreover, a Greek Archaeology paper was included in the syllabus for the reformed final examination, Greats.

There were territorial changes too. The University had decided that its collections of Eastern Art should move into the Ashmolean Museum and occupy the area held there by the casts. With characteristic generosity the University built for the casts a new building, behind the Ashmolean Museum. With characteristic lack of foresight, it provided no direct access to it from the Museum, so that the Gallery is less attended by both the general public and the University than it deserves. And with characteristic canniness it built only two-thirds of it, promising to complete the building later, which of course has never happened. Ashmole designed the layout of the new building, supervised the difficult move and initiated the great programme of cleaning which was required.

I have dwelt on the work of the Professors, because this is the centenary of the Chair. But in Oxford, and Cambridge, of all the universities of the world, it is accepted that professors are not important, but are ignorable, even sometimes expendable. It would be unjust in any brief and even biased review of classical archaeology in Oxford not to say something of other Oxford scholars.

The teaching of classical archaeology has inevitably centred on the Ashmolean Museum. Arthur Evans was its Keeper of Antiquities from 1884 to 1908 and I will not dilate on his worth and influence. Hogarth, excavator of Naucratis and the Temple of Artemis at Ephesus, was its Keeper of Antiquities from 1909 to 1927. On its staff have figured scholars such as Humfry Payne. They all contributed to the image of classical archaeology in Oxford. In teaching, I have mentioned Farnell, Tod, and Myres. In the colleges there have been many tutors with a profound contribution to make to the subject. Collingwood, philosopher and historian of Roman Britain, was one, and there have been many more. When Collingwood came to Oxford, he found that Evans had pushed the history of Greece back into the Bronze Age but, as he remarks in his autobiography, 'the official reaction of Oxford was to cut out of Greek history ... everything down to the first Olympiad', and that Greek history in Oxford remained scissors and paste until the thirties, while Roman history flourished.[22] The banner of Homeric archaeology, hoisted by Myres, was kept aloft by Hilda Lorimer and Dorothea Gray, and now by Mervyn Popham, himself an excavator of Knossos. Nor should we forget Beazley's great friend Paul Jacobsthal who brought to Oxford that style of devoted German scholarship that Beazley and Gardner admired.

In 1927 the University created a Readership in Classical Archaeology, a supporting role to the Professor. Its first holder was Stanley Casson, a scholar as unlike Beazley or Gardner as it is possible to be. The Readers in Classical Archaeology have, probably by accident rather than intention, seemed to provide the alternative archaeology to the mainstream teaching of the Professors. Casson was a traveller, an excavator, a prehistorian, but capable of making a contribution to more conventional classical archaeological studies through his work on sculptural techniques. He was succeeded in 1945 by the brilliant T.J. Dunbabin, historian and excavator. Tom Dunbabin's untimely death in 1955 brought to the post Llewellyn Brown, who had turned to coins and to Etruscan archaeology, but he too was to be taken untimely from a promising career. And the latest of the Readers, Jim Coulton, has at last brought to Oxford a proper study of Greek architecture, which Gardner would have applauded.

This flow of support, from colleges and University, has contributed to the sustained growth of the subject and its diversity. It will not have escaped your attention that in Oxford 'Classical' means Greek. In 1956 a Chair in the Archaeology of the Roman Empire was founded and its first holders, Ian Richmond and Sheppard Frere, directed the teaching mainly to the Roman Provinces. Throughout the past century Roman archaeology, and notably Romano-British studies, have been strongly supported in Oxford, though even after the founding of the Chair, inexplicably, it was some years before they could be found a role in undergraduate studies.

And where are we now? I am not particularly sorry that Oxford is making no very determined or committed contribution to what is called the New Archaeology in the classical sphere. New Archaeology, like *nouvelle cuisine*, is seductive in appearance but nutritionally unsatisfying, and we may do well to be, in the Beazley manner, fastidious in our selection of lost causes, and refuse to be dominated by a school or dogma. In Oxford research subjects are still chosen by the students, not dictated by the professors. But we do not live in the nineteenth century. Since the Research Laboratory for Archaeology and the History of Art was founded in 1955 classical archaeology has been a prominent user, and the Laboratory's first major colony was in the British School at Athens.

The most important new research development derives, very properly, from Beazley. The University purchased from him his collection of photographs and notes, which were left in his care. After his death in 1970 they were brought to the Ashmolean Museum and installed in the Cast Gallery, their natural home. Shortly afterwards Donna Kurtz was appointed Archivist, and thanks to her patience and skill the Archive, backed by the resources of the Ashmolean Library, has become a centre for the study of Athenian vase-painting, much visited by scholars from other universities all over the world. Beazley's contribution to his subject was so overwhelming that it could not be replaced or reworked, it could only be updated. In 1979 a project of computerising and publishing addenda to Beazley's lists, and then of making a computerised database for all Athenian figure-decorated vases, was inaugurated. The British Academy adopted the project in 1981 and it has been significantly helped by Lincoln College and, since 1984, by the J. Paul Getty Trust. It will ensure that the framework for the study erected by Beazley will not falter by becoming outdated, and that the material of a subject which is bibliographically and museographically a mess, but which is of crucial importance to many classical studies, will be under control and accessible world wide.

Gardner would have regarded the computer as the work of the devil. Beazley, I think, would have welcomed it. His fastidiousness, noted by Gardner, being carefully selective, exactly suits the computer, and his whole method of work, recording and publication is translatable directly into computerised information more readily than that of any other scholar of Beazley's generation. But classical archaeology in Oxford has not lost itself in Ariel-like aspirations to throw a girdle round the globe with its technology of information, though it is well on its way to doing just that. The computer terminals and Archive live in the building that houses Gardner's great collection of casts. The numbers of undergraduates and graduates taught exceed by now even Gardner's. And if successive Lincoln Professors have failed to convince the Faculty one hundred per cent that this subject is as vital to the study of Classics as any other, this is perhaps only a minor fault in the record. I leave the last word with Gardner, since in some respects the 1890's seem not so distant from the 1980's:[23]

> If it be asked, what is the connection between classical archaeology and literature, the answer is that the plastic and poetic arts grow from the same root, and send out shoots in the same directions. If it be asked what is the connection between archaeology and history, the answer is that archaeology *is* history, and history of the best kind, very often the only history we shall have.

NOTES

1   R.F. Ovenell's forthcoming book, *The Ashmolean Museum 1683 – 1894* (Oxford, 1986), is an important source and I am indebted to him for notes on early acquisitions of casts in the University. A fund was organised by the Duncans in 1823 to purchase the Fouquet casts of classical architecture, which were placed in the Picture Gallery of the Bodleian Library. In 1835 Philip Duncan presented casts of the Discobolus, the Laocoon and the Apollo Belvedere, with others, to adorn the Radcliffe Camera. In 1884 the University started making annual contributions for the collection of casts. Before Gardner arrived the casts had been moved to the University Galleries (later the Ashmolean Museum) and placed down the centre of its main gallery, and some casts from the adjacent Taylor Institution later joined them. The opening of the new room of casts on 17 October 1890 was announced by Stuart-Jones, Hogarth, Gardner, Farnell and A.C. Clauson. In a letter to Fortnum of 9 October 1894 Arthur Evans writes, 'I find that even Gardner is not trusted to get his own casts without a "Cast Committee" over him which he does not appreciate!' Fortnum, the great benefactor of the Ashmolean, displayed some alarm at the Lincoln Professor's occupancy of so much of the building (letter to Evans, 18 October 1898). I am also indebted to Anne Brown, of the Ashmolean Museum, for information from Evans's letters, and especially the poem, quoted later in this lecture, which is published by kind permission of the Sir Arthur Evans Will Trust.

2   A.J. Engel, *From Clergyman to Don* (1983) gives a good account of nineteenth-century Oxford.

3   On the Arundel marbles in Oxford, see A. Michaelis, *Ancient Marbles in Great Britain* (1882) 538 – 40, 572, 580; D.E.L. Haynes, *The Arundel Marbles* (1975).

4   *Autobiographica* (1933) 59.

5   For the problems of Lincoln College and the Chair, see V. Green, *The Commonwealth of Lincoln College 1427 – 1977* (1979) 500 – 502, 523.

6   Joan Evans, *Time and Chance* (1943) includes an account of Arthur Evans's relations with the Ashmolean, and for his views on the Chair, pp. 261 – 62.

7   From the obituary he wrote for Gardner in *Proceedings of the British Academy* 23 (1937) 459 – 69 (p. 464 cited).

8   See his *Autobiographica*. Gardner died in 1937, aged 91. His predecessor as Lincoln Professor, Ramsay, died in 1939, aged 88. Of his successors, Beazley died aged 85; in 1985 Bernard Ashmole celebrated his 91st birthday, and Martin Robertson his 75th. *Absit omen.*

9   *Catalogue of the Greek Vases in the Ashmolean Museum* (1893), and supplements in *JHS* 24 (1904), 25 (1905). Arthur Evans, writing to Fortnum on 4 May 1891 from Sicily: 'It has been a great satisfaction to me to secure these vases as one of the objects that I have had in view during these last years was to secure a good representative collection of Greek vases of which there was not before more than a beginning and the need of which was the greater as the study of ancient vase painting at Oxford has made great progress under Gardner and is a bridge over which the Classical students are tempted to enter in to [the] field of art.'

10   See Hill (n. 7, above) 467 – 68, quoting Dean Inge's assessment of Gardner's work in this area. And Gardner, *Autobiographica* 74 – 96.

11   Gardner, *New Chapters in Greek Art* (1926) 31 – 32, and *Autobiographica* 57.

12   Some have been exhibited recently by the Benaki Museum in Athens: see *Athens 1839 – 1900: A Photographic Record* (Benaki Museum, 1985).

13   Childe and Evans were admitted to read for the Diploma on 13 October 1914. (On Beazley's effect on them, see D.C. Kurtz in *Occasional Papers on Antiquities* (Getty Museum) 3 (1985) 243.) Beazley had been invited to assist in teaching vases to Diploma candidates on 14 October 1909. Other landmarks recorded in the Minutes of the Committee for Archaeology are the admission of Bernard Ashmole and A.W. Lawrence on 29 April 1919; Beazley's appointment as a Lecturer

on 20 January 1920. 24 January 1922 saw the proposals of the Vice-Chancellor (then L.R. Farnell) for greater recognition of Classical Archaeology in the Literae Humaniores school and the need for a general training in 'cultural aesthetic'. The proposals got nowhere, and an attempt to add Renaissance art to the Diploma was defeated (17 October 1922).

14 *Autobiographica* 36 — 37.

15 *Ibid.* 64 — 65.

16 From Gardner's Introductory (Inaugural) Lecture 'Classical Archaeology, wider and general', delivered on 19 October 1887, p. 14.

17 *New Chapters in Greek Art* ch. 2.

18 *Ibid.* ix.

19 From the Introductory Lecture (n. 16, above) 15, 24.

20 On the young Beazley in Oxford, see the rather colourful account in J. Sherwood, *No Golden Journey* (1973), which quotes some of his verse. He had a poem published in *Oxford Poetry 1910 — 1913* (1913).

21 In a book devoted to select students, he notes: 'Great progress and proficiency: but fastidiousness.' His notes on Exercise papers taken by Beazley for Mods in 1905 read: 'Tutor, C. Bailey. Paper 1 fanciful and vague but interested; Paper 2 very good at seeing points. Paper 1 took pains and compared points; Paper 2 stiff but reads and looks improving.' The overall mark was alpha minus, his highest for any student.

22 R.G. Collingwood, *An Autobiography* (1939) 82 — 83.

23 *Classical Archaeology at Oxford* (1889) 10.

SIR JOHN BEAZLEY (1885–1970)

Bernard Ashmole

LINCOLN PROFESSOR 1956–1961

(reprinted from *The Proceedings of the British Academy* 56 (1970) 443–61)

JOHN DAVIDSON BEAZLEY was born in Glasgow on 13 September 1885, the elder son of Mark John Murray Beazley of London, and Mary Catherine Davidson of Glasgow. His father's father had been born at Ickford in Buckinghamshire, and married Rosanna Holland, a Protestant Irishwoman; his mother's father, John Davidson, was probably from Montrose in Scotland. He learnt much about arts and crafts from his father, who was an interior decorator. His mother, a nurse, was of sterling character, and the mainstay of the family in many vicissitudes.

After the birth of the younger brother, Mark, in 1887, the family moved to Southampton, where in 1896 the two boys went to King Edward VI School. The school magazine for 1898 has an entry 'J.D. Beazley, the youngest boy in form VI, has been elected to Christ's Hospital by open competition'; he seems to have come first among all the entrants. Sixty years later he wrote: 'I never forget how much I owe to Southampton and to the School, above all to H. W. Gidden, kindest and wisest of men, but also Fewings and Holmes and the others who bore with me, taught me, and befriended me.' (Gidden was Classics master, Fewings Head Master, and Holmes Second Master.)

In 1897 his father moved to Brussels to learn the technique of glass-making, taking his wife and younger son with him. John—who throughout his life was called 'Jack' or 'Jacky' by family and friends—remained at Christ's Hospital and visited the family during vacations, until in 1912 they migrated to West Virginia, where his brother managed a glass factory and his father was in charge of one of its departments. His mother died in 1918, his father in 1940, and his brother in 1956; all are buried at Charleston.

The home in Brussels gave him a base from which he was able to travel extensively in Europe—his first recorded journey is a walking-tour with his brother in Champagne, and he took his mother to Italy in 1911—and in Brussels he was first fired with his passion for Greek vases, for he once wrote of the exquisite cup there by Onesimos, depicting a young girl going to the bath, as his 'first vase-love'. It was indeed the first vase he remembered having seen.

At Christ's Hospital, where his classics master was F. H. Merk, once a scholar of Balliol, he was a Classical Grecian, but in his last year he also won prizes for Religious Knowledge, French, and English Essay, and was awarded the Prix de Sans-Souci of the Société Nationale des Professeurs de Français en Angleterre. In

1903 he took first place in the classical scholarship examination at Balliol. Here his tutors were Cyril Bailey and A.W. Pickard-Cambridge. He took firsts in Classical Moderations and Literae Humaniores, and of university prizes and scholarships nearly swept the board—Ireland Scholar and Craven Scholar in 1904; Hertford Scholar in 1905; Derby Scholar in 1907. In that year he also won the Gaisford Prize for Greek prose with 'Herodotus at the Zoo', his first published work, which catches both the style and the mood of Herodotus to perfection, and in the marginal notes gently derides German editors of the classics. It was reprinted for the second time in 1911, and again, in Switzerland, in 1968. His interest in verbal scholarship never flagged; if he had chosen that field it is plain that he would soon have been among the half-dozen leading linguistic scholars in the world, and editors in later years fortunate enough to enlist his aid over their manuscripts or proofs left their readers in no doubt of their debt to him.

Oxford did not immediately recognize his genius. He gave tuition for Moderations as Lecturer at Christ Church in 1907, but when next year his appointment to a permanent Studentship (Fellowship) was discussed, one report, allegedly from someone in Balliol, said that he was 'idle and irresponsible'. His idleness must have consisted in not spending his time on what he knew already, his irresponsibility in devoting it to studies then off the beaten track; for instance, he writes casually to his hostess after a week-end: 'I came back and read three speeches of Demosthenes that I had never clapped eyes on before, one of them quite sordid and amusing.'

In 1908 he was elected Student and Tutor at Christ Church, a post that he held for seventeen years. E.S.G. Robinson knew him at this time, and writes:

> I well remember his private hours. He was only two or three years older than I, and they were very informal. His conversation was brilliant; his presence, as I remember it then, translucent features topped by pale gold hair, was dazzling. He thought it would be amusing to polish up my verse composition; perhaps a reaction from his deliberate abandonment about this time of writing English verse. We took Housman's 'Shropshire Lad' and turned many of its poems into Latin elegiacs. He would go through my copy with skill and kindness, then, in a few minutes, with idiomatic and effortless ease, produce his own version.
>
> Our first meeting, however, was not over Latin elegiacs. In the previous year a wave of pageants—episodes of local history enacted by locals—had swept through the country, and Oxford must have hers like other places. Obviously there was no lack of material, and the result was more successful than most. One of the best episodes was a mediaeval allegory, the Masque of Learning, showing the Good Student and the Bad Student alternately tempted by Folly, with the Seven Deadly Sins, and by War, a splendid knight on horseback; but sustained by the Virtues and the Faculties—Philosophy, Jurisprudence, Geometry &c., led by Divinity. Into this scene suddenly burst Bacchus with his rout of nymphs and satyrs (the flower of North Oxford and the University) wreathed, and clad in fawn-skins. Bacchus, aloft in his golden car, was drawn by two yoked satyrs, one of them J.D. Beazley the other the writer. As Bacchus distributed his treasures to the crowd, students and other hangers-on raised the Goliardic drinking-song *meum est propositum in taberna mori*. It was never quite clear to the writer which side in the end

carried the day, but he will always remember the set face of his yoke-fellow and his grim determination to go through with it.

As an undergraduate Beazley had formed a close friendship with James Elroy Flecker, who was next door at Trinity. Both wrote poetry, and they acted in theatricals together. Beazley published three poems in the *English Review* for April 1911; they are distinguished and sensitive, but with no clear promise of greatness. In later life he would never speak of his poetry, and it was not possible to discover how much he had written or why he had abandoned it.

T.E. Lawrence, in a letter to Sydney Cockerell, wrote: 'Beazley is a very wonderful fellow, who has written almost the best poems that ever came out of Oxford: but his shell was always hard, and with time he seems to curl himself tighter and tighter into it. If it hadn't been for that accursed Greek art, he'd have been a very fine poet.' Flecker also esteemed his poems highly, and when, after college, they drifted apart, addressed to him an 'Invitation to a young but learned friend to abandon archaeology and play once more with his neglected Muse'; but by this time Beazley had turned to what he knew was to be his life's work.

In the very year that he was to take up the Studentship at Christ Church, he and Flecker were stranded penniless in Florence. Flecker was able to get money from his father, and so pay the *pensione* and his train fare. Beazley went to the British Consul and applied for help, but it was rudely refused. The landlady of the *pensione*, however, who was Danish, advanced him the money for his return fare and did not insist on being paid for his room and board; and Beazley was able to reach Oxford, where he was expected to have been teaching, with the minimum of delay. Ever afterwards he held all Danes in high esteem—'very decent people they are'.

His first visit to Cambridge seems to have been in 1904. J.T. Sheppard, in his diary for 1905, several times has the word *Beazley* underlined as though to mark an important event, and Beazley nearly fifty years later told of the impression of cleverness left on his mind by conversation there: 'I thought J.M. Keynes and Lytton Strachey the two cleverest men I had ever met; and looking back over the years I still think they are the two cleverest men I ever met.'

His lifelong friendships with two Fellows of Trinity College, Cambridge, Andrew Gow and Donald Robertson, began about 1909. In 1910 he was with Gow in Paris studying in the Louvre. Concentration on Greek art had not prevented his acquiring an extensive knowledge of other forms of art—Italian and, especially, Flemish painting, and together they bought a little picture which they judged to be by Simone Martini. It was eventually found to be from a polyptych of which other panels had been acquired by Langton Douglas, and believing that the panels ought to be reunited, they sold it to him; it is now in the Lehman Collection (Metropolitan Museum of New York) and is thought to be a copy by Lippo Vanni of a figure by Simone Martini.

There are a number of letters and postcards written in 1911 and 1912 to Donald Robertson and his wife Petica, when Beazley was working in museums in every part of France, Germany, and Italy; St. Petersburg he had also planned to visit, but the Hermitage was shut, and he did not go to Russia until 1914; his first journey to America was in the same year. The correspondence is illustrated with satirical pencil drawings of incidents in his travels, displaying a talent which, had he cared, would have won distinction anywhere; henceforth it was to be devoted to making those hundreds of delicate records of Greek vases which are preserved in his archives in Oxford. The letters describe his identification of various Greek vase-painters and the attribution of vases to them; in one letter, for instance, congratulating the Robertsons on the birth of their son Martin, he says 'I count myself a grandfather. The fortieth child was born to Hermonax yesterday.'

On one of these journeys he met in Munich Karl Reichhold, who was engaged in drawing, for Furtwängler's and Reichhold's great *Griechische Vasenmalerei*, the vase in Boston from which the Pan Painter takes his name. Reichhold told him of E.P. Warren, who had bought the vase for Boston, and soon after Beazley was introduced to Warren in Oxford. Warren in turn introduced him to John Marshall, and at Lewes House in Sussex Beazley was able to study at leisure a whole range of newly found or newly acquired vases, sculptures, and gems, and to enjoy the intellectual stimulus of these two fine scholars and lovers of antiquity. The community at Lewes House has been described by O. Burdett and E.H. Goddard in *Edward Perry Warren* (1941), to which Beazley contributed a chapter on 'Warren as Collector'.

During the First World War he served in Intelligence as a lieutenant of the Royal Naval Volunteer Reserve. When he returned to Oxford he continued to teach in Christ Church, and in 1920 was appointed University Lecturer in Greek Vases. The Lincoln and Merton Professorship of Classical Archaeology was then held by Professor Percy Gardner. When, on his impending retirement, the question of his successor arose, those who recognized Beazley's unique qualities had no doubt who it ought to be, but there was some opposition, partly because he was by some thought too remote to be a good teacher—and no doubt he was better with the better pupils—partly because Percy Gardner, who had fought for many years for the recognition in Oxford of Greek Art as a subject of humane studies, distrusted his 'scientific' approach. However, Beazley was elected to the Chair in 1925, and for thirty years made Oxford the focus of the world for the study of Greek art. He was intensely loyal to Oxford, and many still living will remember that in replying to a speech in his honour at the opening in 1967 of the exhibition of his gifts to the Ashmolean, his one theme was gratitude for its privileges.

It was in Oxford in March 1913 that he first met his future wife Marie, daughter of Bernard Bloomfield. At the end of the First World War they met again: she was now a widow, her husband, David Ezra, having been killed in France. On 13 August 1919, they were married, and later went, with Marie's young daughter, to the Judge's Lodging, the fine eighteenth-century house in St. Giles', which they shared with the sisters Mabel and Ellen Price, the latter an enthusiastic student of Greek vases with whom Beazley collaborated in the second Oxford fascicule of the *Corpus Vasorum*.

Marie was a woman of strong and remarkable character. Dark and exotically handsome, highly intelligent, she had been brought up in cosmopolitan society, mainly in Vienna, Roumania, and Turkey. She had read widely, spoke French,

the family language, with style—German until the Second War but never after—
later also Italian and Spanish; she was an accomplished pianist, and drew with
some talent. Her devotion to Beazley was as complete as his to her, and she
subordinated her own interests entirely, so that he might work everywhere in
comfort and free from interruption; even on their wedding-day he was allowed
after a time to go to the Ashmolean, whilst she continued to entertain the guests.
Dietrich von Bothmer's words cannot be bettered:

> Lady Beazley looked after her husband with a passionate devotion and in a spirit
> of self-denial seldom found in anybody endowed with so strong a character as
> hers. Though raised in an age and environment of unperturbed comfort and
> gracious living, she readily accepted, with all its sacrifices, the world and life of a
> scholar. At Oxford she ran the household, entertained guests, and looked after
> many a burdensome detail; on travels abroad she organized everything, from
> plane tickets to hotels, restaurants and foreign exchange ... During the long hours
> her husband worked in museums she sat by his side, reading, or writing letters,
> and keeping museum curators and museum guards alike engaged in convers-
> ation, thus saving her husband much time.

Although completely inexperienced, she made herself an expert photographer
of Greek vases, one of the most difficult of subjects because of the reflections from
the black glaze and the distortion of the picture by the receding surface of the vase;
the hundreds of photographs on large glass plates that she took in many museums
testify to her skill and to the superiority of patience and honesty over some of the
more specious modern devices.

Some thought it a strange partnership, but were bound to admit that it was
impossible to imagine him married to anyone else. He warmly admired her
accomplishments and never ceased to delight in her company and her conversation; their loving companionship lasted until her death forty-eight years later.
They had no children.

They travelled widely together in the course of his work—to France, Italy,
Greece, Cyprus, Turkey, and Israel. In 1924 they visited Spain, and both were
entranced by Spanish music and dancing and by the Spanish way of life. Just
before the Second World War she invented a knitted cylinder which could be
variously used—as muffler, helmet, body-belt, knee-rug, and otherwise—and
which he aptly named *kredemnon* after the life-saving garment given to Odysseus by
Leucothea. When war broke out she and her friends knitted hundreds of these
which they sent to members of the Forces, especially to seamen and to those
manning the mine-sweepers. Both took a personal interest in the recipients, of
whom a careful list was kept, and letters exchanged.

In 1941 he had declined an invitation to become the Sather Professor at
Berkeley, California, because he did not want to be away from England during the
war, and during the war they would never themselves make use of the numerous
food-parcels sent by admirers abroad. In 1946 he was again invited to the United
States, this time by Dr Gisela Richter, Curator of Greek and Roman Art in the
Metropolitan Museum of New York. Miss Richter had long been a friend and
helper, she had supplied him regularly with photographs of vases, had drawn his

attention to many obscure collections, and had discussed with him many archaeological matters. He stayed for four months, enjoying her companionship and the life of the Department, revisiting the great American collections, interchanging ideas and information with Bothmer, then her assistant, and receiving from him not only friendship, but also help in the many little problems of travel and daily life which, in the absence of his wife, he was ill-equipped to solve. He returned to Oxford much refreshed.

They now resided at 100 Holywell, a rambling house from room after room of which they were gradually squeezed by the apparatus of learning, until they were living in a small breakfast-room, and his work-table was in a dressing-room upstairs, the whole of the ground floor having become a closely packed reference-library of books, drawings, and photographs.

In middle age he began to suffer from attacks of dizziness, and from deafness. The deafness grew steadily worse, and eventually it became impossible to communicate with him except by pencil and paper or by gestures. He retired from the Lincoln Chair in 1956, and was succeeded by Bernard Ashmole, one of his earliest and most faithful admirers.

In 1949 he had accepted the renewed invitation to become the Sather Professor at Berkeley. This had been one of their happiest ventures, and both made many friends; to an old friend there, H.R.W. Smith, he dedicated the publication of the lectures he delivered. His retirement gave him further opportunities for travel, and in 1964 he and Lady Beazley paid a successful visit to Australia and New Zealand under the auspices of A.D. Trendall, who had done much to further Greek studies in the Antipodes, and who was now at Canberra. It was in Australia that he delivered his last public lecture, on a subject he loved, the Berlin Painter.

During the sixties Lady Beazley's health began to fail, and she died after a stroke in 1967. He bore the blow with fortitude, but during the rest of his life chance remarks made it clear that he was constantly thinking of her. After her death he retained the tenancy of 100 Holywell and used it for working, but lived in the Holywell Hotel across the street, where he was well cared for. Although his mind remained clear he became much enfeebled, and was unable to speak or write more than a few words, but he continued to correct proofs, to read new books and to make notes upon them. He walked with difficulty, but took pleasure in the exercise and refused to abandon his visits to the Ashmolean, although these became increasingly perilous. After a very short illness he died peacefully on 6 May 1970.

By then he had received the widest possible recognition, and every honour that the world of learning could confer, accepting them all with modesty but with evident pleasure. He was created a Knight Bachelor in 1949 and a Companion of Honour ten years later. In Oxford, besides being an Honorary Student of Christ Church, and an Honorary Fellow of Balliol and of Lincoln College, he had been made an Honorary Doctor of Letters in 1956. Elsewhere in Britain, he had been honoured by degrees at Cambridge, Glasgow, Durham, and Reading; abroad, at Marburg, Lyons, Paris, and Thessalonike. He had been a Fellow of the British Academy since 1927, and in 1957 became the first holder of its Kenyon medal. He was an Honorary Vice-President of the Greek Archaeological Society, Foreign

Associate of the Académie des Inscriptions et Belles-Lettres, Foreign Member of the American Philosophical Society, Philadelphia, of the Pontificia Accademia Romana, of the Royal Danish Academy, of the Athens Academy, and of the Austrian Academy. He was also an Honorary Fellow of the Metropolitan Museum of New York, and Honorary Member of the Archaeological Institute of America and of the Accademia dei Lincei, which in 1965 awarded him the Antonio Feltrinelli Foundation Prize.

Beazley had several pupils, several devoted disciples from other universities, and a host of followers; all these profited by the fruits of his labours and applied his methods with varying degrees of judgement. Humfry Payne became interested in Greek art during his last year as an undergraduate at Christ Church, and after graduating in 1924 studied abroad for a couple of years, then became a Senior Scholar of Christ Church and an Assistant Keeper at the Ashmolean Museum, and, in 1929, Director of the British School at Athens. He collaborated with Beazley in an article on the sherds from Naucratis and in a fascicule of the *Corpus Vasorum*; in 1931 he published *Necrocorinthia*, a comprehensive and masterly study of archaic Corinthian art, and, just before his untimely death in 1936, *Archaic Marble Sculpture from the Acropolis*, which contains the most sensitive study of archaic Greek sculpture ever written in English. This was an outstanding mind brought to its finest temper by Beazley's tuition and example. Beazley never ceased to feel his loss, and speaks of him in the *Dictionary of National Biography* in terms that might well be applied to himself: 'a fine eye, deep respect for the individual object, great structural power, wealth of detail combined with breadth of vision, perfect clearness of thought and expression'. Two other distinguished pupils who died before their time were T.J. Dunbabin, Beazley's Reader (senior lecturer) at Oxford, and Llewellyn Brown, who succeeded Dunbabin. Because he was undemonstrative and because he wrote with scholarly restraint, Beazley was sometimes thought to be lacking in warmth; his obituary of Payne and his Foreword to Brown's *The Etruscan Lion*, which is also an obituary, show the falsity of this view.

Another pupil is Dietrich von Bothmer, whose talents came to perfection under his guidance. 'The name of Dietrich von Bothmer', he wrote in the preface to his *Attic Black-figure Vase-painters* of 1956, 'often occurs in these pages, for many ascriptions were first made by him: but he has contributed very much besides: all sorts of information on the whereabouts of vases; on obscure publications; above all, on pieces unknown to me or insufficiently known. I have asked him countless questions, and he has never failed me.' And again in the preface to the second edition of *Attic Red-figure Vase-painters*:

> The red-figure book owes even more to him than the black-figure did. For many years, with the utmost generosity, he has continued to place his notes and photographs at my disposal. Without them many of the vases would be less well-known to me, and many others would not have been known to me at all; many vases, and indeed whole collections, especially in France, America and eastern Europe. He has found time, from a busy life, to read both the manuscript and the proofs; he has supplied me with countless facts about locations, provenances,

obscure publications, and other matters; and by his patient scrutiny and his acute criticisms he has substantially improved the book.

Bothmer wrote an excellent obituary notice in the *Oxford Magazine* for 12 June 1970, part of which is quoted above. He also helped Beazley constantly with his last great work *Paralipomena*, material which had accrued since the publication of his vast reference-book on vases.

Noël Oakeshott is a pupil who (at first as Noël Moon) has done fine work, especially on early South Italian vase-painting. She married Walter Oakeshott, who became Rector of Lincoln College, to which Beazley's Professorship was attached. They were warm friends to the Beazleys; the College welcomed and honoured him; and after Lady Beazley's death both did much for his comfort.

Of Cambridge disciples, A.D. Trendall has applied his methods with great success to the vast field of South Italian vase-painting, and C.M. Robertson, son of his early Cambridge friends and now his successor at Oxford, has carried on the pure tradition, and has devoted many months of work to completing and seeing through the Press *Paralipomena*, which was only in its penultimate stage at Beazley's death. Robertson has also written profound appreciations of him in the *Journal of Hellenic Studies* for 1965, when reviewing the second edition of *Attic Red-figure Vase-painters*, and in the *Burlington Magazine* for August 1970.

It is a commonplace that Beazley revolutionized the whole study of Greek vase-painting, and helped other scholars to an incalculable degree by his published writings. There were other ways, more direct but less well known, in which he aided them. He was constantly consulted, by letter and in person, by scholars and by owners of Greek vases from all over the world. He answered these hundreds of inquiries with courtesy and generosity, withholding none of his knowledge and replying at length in his own careful hand, without the aid of typewriter or secretary. This generosity was occasionally exploited, never, so far as one can remember, by scholars—though perhaps even they sometimes did not acknowledge their full indebtedness—but now and then by dealers, who made use of his attributions to enhance the value of their wares. He would never accept fees for these professional opinions, but was once or twice heard to complain mildly when they failed even to acknowledge his replies.

In the course of his work, and as an essential instrument of it, he built up a body of photographs, drawings, and notes on vases surpassing that of any institution in the world; and these passed at his death to the University of Oxford. His complete library, with an unrivalled collection of offprints, he bequeathed: the other material had been acquired by the University some years before, with the proviso that he should have the use of it as long as he lived. These 'Beazley Archives', now in the Ashmolean, consist of approximately seventy thousand mounted photographs, providing substantial photographic coverage for *ABV* and *ARV* and for much besides; many thousand photographs of sculpture, and many hundreds of unmounted photographs; some hundreds of drawings of whole vases; and, finally, several hundred thousand small sheets of fine paper, uniform in size, filled with notes on vases, usually with details of them drawn or traced in pencil.

Oxford has yet another reason to be grateful. Gifts of antiquities to the Ashmolean had been made steadily for over fifty years, and the Exhibition of 1966, when he gave the large residue of his collection, was a selection from more than eight hundred objects, ranging from vases and small bronzes of the first rank to sherds and smaller antiquities—none without interest—that he and Lady Beazley had given. Partly through dealers consulting him, partly by study of sale-catalogues, he usually knew in good time when an object was coming on to the market, and could often secure it, or, when it was beyond his means, advise the Museum to secure it, at its first appearance in the sale-room, or even before. He also received many vases as presents. Though never a wealthy man, he was able in this way to enrich the Museum with gifts worth many thousands of pounds, and, for teaching, inestimably more. On his sixty-fifth birthday admirers from many countries had dedicated to him a volume of the *Journal of Hellenic Studies*, together with a list of his published writings. The catalogue of the Exhibition brought this list up to date; it contains no fewer than two hundred and seventy-five publications. Though some are short, most are not; and all, whether short or long, are written in the same crisp style, with great felicity of phrase, and with the same perfect scholarship.

Beazley's methods have often been described. He was familiar with Giovanni Morelli's system—itself not completely new—by which the identity of Italian painters could be established through a study of details, especially those constantly recurring details such as the ears, eyes, and hands, for which the artist develops a formula that he is then apt to repeat almost unconsciously, as with a written signature. Morelli claimed for his method the validity of a quasi-scientific experiment, and applied it with a success that must, however, have depended equally on an assessment of the general character and quality of the picture as a work of art. Difficulties arise in that these formulae can easily be imitated by pupils or others, and that the artist himself may modify them with age or change of eyesight, but the underlying assumption is sound enough, and Bernard Berenson used Morelli's method widely on Italian painting. Beazley extended it systemati-cally to Greek vase-painting, which in several ways is more susceptible. The linear technique, which changed little over the years, lends itself more readily than brush-strokes to comparatively simple formulae, not only for eyes, ears, and other anatomical details, but also for many details of drapery; and although there is virtually no literary evidence for the identity of Greek vase-painters, and although signatures are few and often not so easily interpreted as appears at first sight, Greek vases in pristine condition are numerous except in certain old collections, and even there any repainting is obvious in a way that it is not in oil, fresco, or tempera. Finally, there are two other features open to analysis—the decorative details, especially the borders, and the shapes of the vases: the first Beazley explored completely, the second he left partly to others.

Adolf Furtwängler, Paul Hartwig, and Friedrich Hauser had all studied Greek vases with acumen; Beazley owed something to all three, especially to Furtwän-gler, but his concentration on limited objectives within a rapidly accumulating store of knowledge, and his feeling for the subtle differences of individual styles,

soon led to new and far-reaching discoveries. His first major article, published in
1910, was on Kleophrades; his second, in 1911, which he described in a
contemporary letter as 'a model of conciseness carried ad absurdum', was on the
Master of the Berlin Amphora, afterwards renamed the Berlin Painter, one of the
greatest of all Greek vase-painters and perhaps Beazley's favourite among the
many hundreds he came to know. During the next few years there appeared a
series of articles on various painters, consisting chiefly of lists of vases which he
attributed to them and brief studies of their artistic character. That the painters
range from the highest to the lowest is symptomatic, for the master-plan, of which
these were constituent pieces, was nothing less than the identification of all the
painters of Attic red-figured vases, great and humble alike; to that task and to the
parallel study of painters using the black-figured technique, Beazley devoted his
life, although he found time for other fields, and produced there enough to have
been the life-work of any other scholar.

What he had achieved so far was distilled into his *Attic Red-figured Vases in
American Museums*, published under difficulties in the United States in the last year
of the First World War, and dedicated appropriately to E.P. Warren and John
Marshall, who had built up the great collections in America. It is not an attractive
book. The binding is in black and terra-cotta, a colour-combination, supposedly
echoing that of the vases, which Beazley disliked; some of the contours of the vases
are painted round by the block-makers, a practice which he detested; the line-
blocks coarsen his fine pencil-drawings; the print is rather small for the large page,
and the text is broken up by lists of vases and by pictures on various scales inserted
here and there. Yet the book is valuable beyond compare, and will so remain; it is
in effect a history of Attic red-figured vase-painting, unequalled for clarity of
exposition, written round the vases in America, but containing a wealth of new
material from other collections everywhere, and defining the personality of the
painters with a precision that had never been approached before.

The preface sets out its aim with a characteristic blend of self-confidence and
modesty:

> I have tried to find out who painted each [vase]. I have not been able to assign
> every vase to its author, although I do not consider that an impossible task, but I
> have managed to put in place most of the more, many of the less, important
> pieces. ... I neither expect that all my attributions will be unhesitatingly accepted
> nor wish that they should. Some of them will be self-evident, most of them require
> to be studied or checked.

There then follows a simple explanation of the method, and finally of its
difficulties:

> There is always danger, of course, of mistaking for the master's work what is really
> a close imitation by a pupil or companion; of mistaking for the pupil's work what
> is a late, a careless, or an erratic work by the master; of confounding two closely
> allied artists. One or other of these things must have happened more than once in
> the following pages: but I believe that most of what I have written will stand; and
> when I have felt doubt I have expressed it.

Anyone who wishes to grasp the essentials of the study of Greek vases can still not do better than read those few hundred words, written by one who was then only thirty-three years old.

E.P. Warren had invited Beazley to catalogue the ancient gems that later formed the nucleus of the collection in Boston, and in 1920 appeared *The Lewes House Collection of Ancient Gems*, generously acknowledging his debt to Furtwängler, and dedicated to his friend Andrew Gow who had worked on it with him. Here he showed the same acute perception and the same sensitive appreciation as he had displayed in his studies of vases, and the book is indispensable for anyone undertaking work on the subject.

He continued year by year to gather material and to publish articles and reviews, mainly on vases; in 1925 came the first of his encyclopaedic works, in German, *Attische Vasenmaler des rotfigurigen Stils*. Here the character of each painter is described in a few lines—sometimes in a few words—and there follows a list of his vases. This is conciseness indeed, for within five hundred octavo pages some hundred and fifty painters are distinguished, and no less than ten thousand vases are assigned to them.

A foil to these and to the other vast reference-books he was later to produce is a series of charming lectures marked by a limpid style, extraordinary perceptiveness, quiet humanity, and a complete absence of the verbiage that commonly enshrouds the history of art. *Attic Black-figure: a Sketch* (1928); *Attic White Lekythoi* (1937); and *Potter and Painter in Ancient Athens* (1944) are examples of these. His chapters on archaic and classical painting and sculpture for volumes IV, V, and VI of the *Cambridge Ancient History* (published afterwards as a book *Greek Sculpture and Painting*) again illustrate these qualities, and his easy command of the whole field of Greek art. He did not, however, love all its manifestations equally, and the chapters on Hellenistic art were written by Ashmole.

Greek Vases in Poland appeared in 1928. It is similar to *Vases in America*, except that South Italian, and Attic black-figure as well as red-figure are included. In the two-year interval he had also produced a fascicule of the *Corpus Vasorum*, his chapters for the *Cambridge Ancient History*, a number of reviews, an elegant translation of E. Pfuhl's *Masterpieces of Greek Drawing and Painting*, and an article on the Antimenes Painter, an important master of Attic black-figure. In 1931 he co-operated with his friend L.D. Caskey, Curator of the Department of Classical Art in the Boston Museum, to produce Part I of the catalogue of *Attic Vase-Paintings in the Museum of Fine Arts, Boston*. (Parts II and III were completed after Caskey's death by Beazley alone in 1954 and 1963.) In the meantime he had found time to write two admirable monographs on the Berlin Painter and the Pan Painter in a series *Bilder Griechischer Vasen* which he and his friend Paul Jacobsthal had initiated. To these he added a third, on the Kleophrades Painter, in 1933.

Campana Fragments in Florence, published in the same year, mostly at his own expense, is an extraordinary production. Thousands of fragments of Greek vases from Campana's 'Collection' had been acquired by the Museum of Florence in 1871 and had lain unheeded in boxes for forty years, after which there had been one or two half-hearted attempts at publication. Beazley worked through them all and joined what could be joined among them, but his unique knowledge enabled him to make joins also with vases in other collections, and the frontispiece of the book shows a cup by Oltos which is put together from sherds in Rome, Florence, Heidelberg, Brunswick, Baltimore, and Bowdoin College. At first sight this looks like a jig-saw puzzle miraculously completed, and so it is, but the miracle consists, not so much in remembering the shape of the gaps to be filled, as in being able to recognize an individual artist in even the smallest fragment. The illustrations consist mainly of seventeen large sheets of thin paper, bearing diagrams of the fragments that join each other, and Beazley writes 'seventeen flimsies are an austere mode of illustration. I have mitigated them by the addition of three collotype plates, but even so I doubt whether my book will ever be really popular.' And he mocks not unkindly at a scholar who previously worked on the fragments, and who gives only four numbers on a plate illustrating a hundred and six of them: 'he has been extraordinarily economical of numbers: and yet they are so cheap! and mathematicians tell us that there is an almost inexhaustible supply of them!'

To most people the name Beazley immediately suggests Athenian vases, and they are apt to ignore his other interests, which were wide. He had constantly been concerned with Etruscan art, and in 1947 published *Etruscan Vase-painting* in the series of Oxford Monographs in Classical Archaeology which he had started with Paul Jacobsthal and of which they were joint editors. It is, and will continue to be, the standard work on the subject. He followed it in 1950 with a delightful and vastly illuminating essay on 'The World of the Etruscan Mirror'.

The Sather Lectures on 'The Development of Attic Black-figure' made a profound impression on those who heard them at Berkeley. Their publication in 1951 was a disaster, chiefly because Beazley was travelling at the time, and the Press concerned printed them without his seeing the proofs, and with the illustrations trimmed and doctored in a way that he would never have permitted. His ferocious comments on these procedures, though amusing, were tokens of real distress, and he continued to be unhappy about it until a corrected edition was published thirteen years later.

Attische Vasenmaler of 1925 seemed at the time, and was, a gigantic achievement, but it was dwarfed in 1942 by *Attic Red-figure Vase-painters* (universally known as *ARV*) which identified no less than three hundred new painters and gave detailed lists of their vases. The second edition, of 1963, dealt with more than seven hundred painters. 'It need hardly be said that the difference between this edition and the last is not in numbers only; every piece has been reconsidered many times.' The magnitude of this achievement and its value cannot be enhanced by words, or even adequately described, but every student of Greek art is aware of them, and the further and deeper he goes the more he realizes his debt. In the meantime there had appeared, in 1956, with a dedication to the memory of his mother, *Attic Black-figure Vase-painters (ABV)*, which treated the black-figured on the same system as the red-figured, identified five hundred potters and painters, and attributed to them some ten thousand vases. As if this were not enough, Beazley continued to keep a list of every new vase that came into his ken, fitted it into the framework of *ARV* and *ABV*, and with characteristic generosity lodged copies of the list with the

Ashmolean Museum in Oxford, the Metropolitan Museum of Art in New York, and the Agora Museum in Athens. These *Paralipomena* continued to be gathered to within a few months of his death, and by the devoted labours of Dietrich von Bothmer and Martin Robertson have now been published; the volume is not much smaller than *ABV* in size, of comparable value, and equally indispensable.

The occasional shafts of wit that lighten the two or three thousand pages of these great works of reference are not always easy to find among the lists of vases, but the 'Instructions for Use' which appear after the preface in both *ARV* and *ABV* give a readier yield: 'My attributions have often been misquoted. In the *Corpus Vasorum*, for example, misquotation appears to be the rule, although I do not know that it has been anywhere prescribed in black and white.' Another passage displays perfectly the balance of his mind and the delicacy of his scholarship:

> I may perhaps be allowed to point out that I make a distinction between a vase by a painter and a vase in his manner; and that 'manner', 'imitation', 'following', 'school', 'circle', 'group', 'influence', 'kinship' are not, in my vocabulary, synonyms. The phrase 'in the style of' is used by some where I should write 'in the manner of': this has warrant, but I was brought up to think of 'style' as a sacred thing, as the man himself. I am conscious that the vases placed under the heading 'manner of' an artist are not always in the same category the list may include (1) vases which are like the painter's work but can safely be said not to be from his hand, (2) vases which are like the painter's work but about which I do not know enough to say that they are not from his hand, (3) vases which are like the painter's work, but of which, although I know them well, I cannot say whether they are from his hand or not. Sometimes I make the situation clear, but more often I do not, for the reason that it would be long and tedious to explain just how much I know about each piece, even if I always knew how much I know and do not know.

His writings are full of profound and memorable thoughts; a single example of light but penetrating wit will be appreciated by everyone who has worked on Greek vases and is aware of the tiresome little problem of nomenclature: 'I have used the word "pot" to signify a vase which is not a cup; a better word can be easier imagined than discovered.'

In conversation also his wit was dry, and could be devastating, perhaps the more so because he spoke sincerely but without passion; many will remember, at meetings, some single sentence that put an end to debate. He was scrupulously fair in his judgement of people; and his remark on a colleague notable for a handsome head and a small mouth—'from his little mouth drop little adders'—was intended as a simple observation. He was not without strong dislikes; among them were coloured illustrations of antiquities, and anything that distorted or misrepresented the true appearance of ancient art; even prejudices—against most of the pre-Raphaelites, for instance—and when repairs in the Ashmolean compelled him to pass through the Oriental galleries in order to reach the Library, his haste was evident.

His linguistic abilities were amazing. French, German, Spanish, and Italian he spoke fluently; Danish, Dutch, and modern Greek moderately, and he had a reading knowledge of Turkish and Russian. During the First War, when he was asked at a naval interviewing board whether he knew Serbian, he replied that he would need a fortnight to learn it; this was no boast, merely a statement of fact. When convalescing in his seventies from an attack of pneumonia, he was sitting up in bed reading through Lewis and Short's *Latin Dictionary*. He explained that he had never had time to do so systematically before; that his tutor at Balliol had once recommended it, but at that time he had managed only to read through Liddell and Scott. 'It is amazing', he added, 'how much one doesn't know.' Dietrich von Bothmer also recalls finding him, late in life, when he thought of going back to Russia, working steadily through a Russian dictionary and making a note of every word with which he was not acquainted. His memory often seemed incredible because it was not the mechanical memory of a prodigy, but ruminative—the memory of a humanist. He could quote, and quote with relevance and scholarly accuracy, much of the world's great poetry in many languages, and there was no subject, except perhaps music, which he could not illuminate.

He was an admirer of French tragedy, and enjoyed the light-hearted farces of Labiche and Courteline, but he had besides a taste for robust, simple humour, and Surtees was an author he enjoyed; he called the classical text he usually kept beside him to read at odd moments his 'Mogg', in reference to 'Mogg's ten thousand Cab Fares' carried for reading-matter on fox-hunting visits by Mr Soapey Sponge.

His industry and power of concentration, like his memory, verged on the incredible. When a young graduate, he enjoyed the cinema—silent in those days— watching cricket, or even walking about Oxford—though not so much in the country, where he seemed uneasy—and these would give him an hour or two's respite from work. Later on he would be at his desk from morning to night, day after day, either at home or in the library of the Ashmolean; yet however much absorbed, he would always set aside a little period in the evening to spend with his wife.

He was of medium height, of slight and elegant build, with handsome, sensitive features, rather deep-set blue eyes, and a delicate, almost translucent complexion. He had fine hands, and his way of handling an antiquity was a lesson not only in manners, but in attitude to life. He was gentle and courteous, and although, like many deaf people, he suffered both from the disability and from a series of ineffectual appliances intended to relieve it, he never complained. In youth he could be very gay, and until his hearing failed was the best of company; to the end he was always alert and friendly when greeted; otherwise his look was usually thoughtful and, when he became completely deaf, remote.

His integrity was complete; he always had a clear feeling of what was right, and would speak for it fearlessly. He was without doubt a genius, but a genius whose dominant motive was a sense of duty; he seemed always to be conscious of the need to make the fullest use of time, and of his talents, in the pursuit of truth. Never a finer scholar, or a truer man.

I gratefully acknowledge help from Mr M.W. Barker, Dr D. von Bothmer, the late Sir Maurice Bowra, Mrs M. Donnelly, Sir John Forsdyke, Mr Andrew Gow, Mr A.J. Holland, Dr and Mrs Walter Oakeshott, Professor C.M. Robertson, Dr E.S.G. Robinson, and the Clerk of Christ's Hospital.